William Wyatt Gill

The south Pacific and New Guinea

Past and Present

William Wyatt Gill

The south Pacific and New Guinea
Past and Present

ISBN/EAN: 9783337181024

Printed in Europe, USA, Canada, Australia, Japan

Cover: Foto ©ninafisch / pixelio.de

More available books at **www.hansebooks.com**

Published by Authority of the New South Wales Commissioners
for the World's Columbian Exposition, Chicago, 1893.

THE

SOUTH PACIFIC AND NEW GUINEA

PAST AND PRESENT;

WITH

NOTES ON THE HERVEY GROUP, AN ILLUSTRATIVE SONG
AND VARIOUS MYTHS.

BY

The Rev. WILLIAM WYATT GILL, B.A. (Lon.);
LL.D. (St. Andrews).

Sydney:
CHARLES POTTER, GOVERNMENT PRINTER, PHILLIP-STREET.
1892.
[1s.]

24 89—92

THE SOUTH PACIFIC AND NEW GUINEA.

DISCOVERY.

Vasco Nuñez de Balboa was the first European who, from a mountain-top in the Isthmus of Panama (September 29, 1513), gazed upon the vast expanse of water now known as the Pacific Ocean. Seven years afterwards, Magellan entered (from the strait which now bears his name) the calm waters of that new sea on which he was the first to sail, and which he named the Pacific Ocean (*Mar Pacifico*). Sir Francis Drake entered the Pacific September, 1577, being the first Englishman to sail upon it. Tasman, Roggewein, Dampier, and other explorers of the seventeenth century discovered Australia, New Zealand, Tasmania, and many smaller groups of islands. The voyages of Anson, Behring, the two Bougainvilles, the illustrious Cook, La Perouse, D'Entrecasteaux, Carteret, Vancouver, Kruzenstern, Kotzebue, Commodore Wilkes, &c., &c., practically completed the geographical exploration of the Pacific Ocean. Within recent years several scientific exploring expeditions have examined the Pacific. Of these, the voyages of the "Challenger," "Gazelle," and "Tuscarora" are the most important.

The principal groups—extending from the equator to about 30° south of it—are the following. The Marquesas Islands, the Tuamotu Archipelago, the Society Islands, the Hervey Islands, the Samoan Islands, the Tokelau, Phœnix, and Ellice Groups, the Tongan Group, the Fiji Islands, the Loyalty Islands, the New Hebrides Group, the Santa Cruz Islands, and the Solomon Group.

FORMATION.

Some of these islands are volcanic in their origin; others are coralline. The volcanic islands are mostly very high in proportion to their size. The lofty peaks, or truncated cones, which form their backbone—exquisitely draped with lianas, small shrubs, ferns, and club-mosses—present a most attractive appearance to the voyager.

The coral islands may be divided into three classes, viz., atolls, barrier reefs, and fringing reefs. Atolls are rings of coral reef surrounding a central lagoon of considerable depth. Barrier reefs differ from the atolls chiefly in the fact of their containing an island in the centre, the island being separated from the reef by a body of deep water. Striking examples of this occur amongst the Society and Samoan Groups. Fringing reefs are coralline foundations attached to a volcanic backbone (as at Rarotonga), without any interior deep-water channel.

These marvellous structures are the work of the reef-building coral polype, which however does not live and work below about 120 feet. With respect to the atolls, Dr. Darwin believes that the lagoon is precisely in the place which the top of a shoal, or the highest part of an island, once occupied. In 1888, Mr. John Murray published a new theory of coral island formation, which claims to account for all the phenomena without calling in the aid of subsidence. With this new theory the writer heartily agrees.

A

DESCRIPTION.

The true coral islands, or atolls, are very unattractive, rising only 10 or 15 ft. above high-water mark. The soil consists merely of sand and broken coral, washed on to the reefs by Old Ocean. In this wretched soil grow luxuriantly the coco-nut palm, the screw pine, *Cordia*,* *Hernandia*, *Calophyllum inophyllum*, with a few other lofty forest trees and low shrubs. Sea-going canoes, carefully preserved from generation to generation, are made out of the *Cordia*, the wood of the *Calophyllum* being too hard to be hollowed out with their ancient shell† adzes. So poor is the vegetation of these atolls that not more than fifty species of plants have been found in the Tokelau, Ellice, and Gilbert Groups. All the species consist of littoral plants found on the volcanic islands.

The fauna of these atolls consists chiefly of a few birds, lizards, small brown rats, and insects.

On approaching one of them, the eye rests upon a forest of coco-nut palms rising apparently out of the ocean ; so abundantly does this invaluable palm—the staff of life to thousands of Polynesians—grow on these tropical sand-banks, the roots (in many instances) laved by the sea. In three atolls known to me, the lagoons are of *fresh* water, thereby enabling the inhabitants to cultivate successfully the food-plants of the volcanic islands. The singular circumstance of a large body of fresh water, marked off from the ocean by only half-a-mile of coral reef, may be thus accounted for ; these atolls are believed to be situated over the craters of former volcanoes, and there must be a submarine connection between them and some of the volcanic islands where mountain streams are abundant.

These atolls suffer much from drought. I have known a drought on one of them (Arorae) to last for eight years. On these atolls the natives obtain brackish water by digging in the sand and coral. The water (misnamed "milk") of the coco-nut is therefore highly valued. Happily, the lagoons and surrounding ocean are alive with fish easily caught. As, however, experience proves that it is impossible to sustain life for any length of time on fish only, in times of drought and consequent famine, the natives fell coco-nut palms and eat the crown, which is very palatable. Even the green fronds and roots are pounded and the sap eagerly sucked, in order to counteract the evils resulting from an exclusively fish diet. As might be expected, the natives of Arorae were mere skeletons, and their naturally dark-brown skin became almost black. On a subsequent visit, when abundant rains had fallen, I was glad to see the natural colour restored to their (comparatively) plump bodies.

Several elevated coral islands are found in the South Pacific. Evidently they have been lifted up by successive stages and sudden movements. The islands of Maré, Lifu. Uvéa, Niué, &c, are of this order. On these there are clear indications of three distinct upheavals, which took place at very long intervals. These islands are old enough to have a considerable depth of vegetable soil, covered with coco-nut and other trees, yet not comparable with the volcanic islands for fertility. The cliffs are pierced by large caverns, formerly used as cemeteries, or as places of refuge for the vanquished in battle. Scores of these caves are filled with mummies. Stalactite and stalagmite abound, and form thick and fast-growing layers of lime-rock. I have sometimes chipped off pieces of lime-rock embedding human bones. It is perfectly well understood amongst the natives what tribes or families have the right to use these caverns. I have, with the assistance of native guides and candle-nut torches, explored numbers of them, and have often been

* The wood is brown, beautifully veined with black.
† The ordinary basaltic adze of the volcanic islands not being procurable on the atolls.

amazed at the dazzling beauty suddenly revealed by our flambeaux. At other times the only possible track would terminate abruptly on the edge of an awful chasm or a subterranean stream.

The largest and most celebrated cavern I have explored is "The Labyrinth" (Tuatini), on the island of Mangaia. Anatakotake, on the island of Atiu, will well repay the trouble of exploration. Some very romantic stories are connected with it.

As might be expected, the flora and fauna of the elevated coral islands are less rich than that of the volcanic islands, but much richer than that of the atolls. But whilst most of the species are identical with those found on the neighbouring volcanic islands, there are some interesting local variations arising from changed surroundings.

The volcanic islands have been the theme of admiration of all voyagers, from Cook downwards. It is impossible for one who has spent his days amid the quiet beauties of the temperate zone to conceive of the wealth and variety of vegetation in the tropics. In some parts of New Guinea and the South Pacific I have gazed upon scenes of loveliness that beggar description. Sailing round Tahiti after a heavy tropical downpour, I counted twenty-four waterfalls in the bosom of the mountains, where the foot of man had scarcely ever trod. The full blaze of the morning sun made the streams shine as molten silver against a background of richest green of manifold tints.

PRODUCTS.

Bread-fruit, plantains, bananas of many varieties, the papaw apple, orange, citron, lime, custard-apple, chesnut, guava, mango, pine-apple, and coffee abound. Horses, cattle, goats, pigs, turkeys, fowls, and ducks have been successfully introduced. The honey-bee thrives. In many of the volcanic islands "taro" (*Caladium petiolatum*), plantains, and bananas constitute the staff of life; in others, the yam (*Dioscorea sativa*) and breadfruit (*Artocarpus incisa*) ; in others. again the sweet potato and the papaw apple. The chesnut (*Inocarpus edulis*), the *Alocasia Indica* (*Seeman*), and arrowroot (*Tacca pinnatifida*) are much used. The kava, a narcotic drink much in request on many islands, is prepared (by chewing) from the root of a pepper (*Piper methysticum*).

FAUNA.

The indigenous fauna of the South Pacific is poor in mammals, but rich in birds. Mammals are represented by pigs, dogs, rats, and bats. Pigeons and doves are abundant. The *Megapodius Brenchleyii* is a native of the Solomon Islands. The kagu (*Rhiconetus jubatus*), a peculiar " wingless" bird, has its habitat on New Caledonia only. In Samoa that remarkable bird the tooth-billed pigeon, or little dodo (*Didunculus stringirostris*), is found. The didunculus is the nearest of kin to the extinct dodo. Non-venomous snakes are found on Savaii, and on many islands westward of Samoa. Insects, especially beetles and butterflies, are very plentiful. A spectre insect (*Lopaphus coccophagus*) spends its life exclusively upon the leaflets (the rough inner side) of the coco-nut palm, and is most destructive.

NEW GUINEA.

The flora of New Guinea is extremely rich, but has a closer affinity to that of Australia than to that of the Pacific. *Eucalypti*, acacias, and other Australian types are found from the Gulf of Papua to Humboldt Bay. Various kinds of *Ficus, Casuarina, Araucaria, Colophyllum, Aleurites*, &c., &c., &c., abound. In the mountains oaks, rhododendrons, &c., grow.

In the swamps of New Guinea, especially in the Gulf of Papua, the invaluable sago-palm grows without cultivation. When about twelve years of age, it sends up an immense terminal spike of flowers ; but the fruit is nearly three years in ripening. The tree then gradually withers. The pith is often eaten raw by the natives. The entire pith of this palm is cut into pieces about 3 feet in length, and carefully covered with fibrous matting, for the use of voyagers. But more frequently a coarse sort of arrowroot is prepared from the pith. This enables the women to provide the household with palatable cakes from time to time. To obtain sago in exchange for pottery is the grand object of the great annual expeditions made from Port Moresby to the Gulf of Papua.

The coco-nut palm is plentiful in some parts of New Guinea ; in others infrequent and barren, compared with what I have been accustomed to see in the Pacific. The Areca palm is very abundant ; the nuts are in great request. In many parts of the bush it shoots up straight as a reed, slender and graceful, without any care being taken of it. An inferior species of bread-fruit is common. Numerous varieties of yam are extensively and admirably cultivated. Bananas are plentiful. Strangely enough, the arrow-root plant (*Tacca*), although growing profusely in some places (sandy soils), was never utilised, being looked upon as poisonous. The betel-pepper (*Chavica*), a liana of climbing habit, is obtained in great lengths in the forest. It is sometimes planted by the natives at the base of a lofty tree growing near their huts. Tobacco of excellent quality is indigenous. It is a singular circumstance that the candle-nut (*Aleurites triloba*), which is common in New Guinea, was never used to give light in their dwellings at night.

The writer had the honor of introducing to science a new Papuan Bassia, yielding a delicious fruit. It grows in the south-eastern part of New Guinea, and has been named by Baron von Mueller the *Bassia Erskineana*.

The wild hog (*Sus Papuensis*) is the largest and, excepting the dingo, almost the only true mammal in New Guinea ; all the rest being marsupials. The tusks of the boars are highly valued as mouth ornaments in battle. Two pairs are firmly tied together and held between the teeth. Among the marsupials are a tree kangaroo, a grey flying opossum, and several cuscus. There are two spiny ant-eaters (*Echidna*) in New Guinea. In 1884 I secured a specimen of the *Tachyglossus Lawesii*. Mr. W. H. Caldwell has lately shown that both *Echidnas* are oviparous, producing a single egg at a birth. This interesting discovery supplies the connecting link between reptiles and mammalia.

The wealth and beauty of the avifauna are great. Dr. Ramsay, of Sydney, gives about fifty-five species, belonging to twenty genera, of the gorgeous Birds of Paradise, all peculiar to New Guinea and the adjacent islands, excepting three species belonging to the genus *Ptilorhis*, found in Australia.

Of 1,028 species of birds, belonging to 321 genera, for the Papuan sub-region, 470 are said to be peculiar to New Guinea and the neighbouring islands, including Aru. The most remarkable orders, excluding the above-mentioned Birds of Paradise, are the honeysuckers, flycatchers, parrots, kingfishers, and pigeons, all rich in special forms. There are in New Guinea no vultures, pheasants, woodpeckers, or finches. We shot several fine brown hawks, very destructive to poultry.

Of all bird-dwellings, the most singular I have seen is that of the *Megapodius* of New Guinea and the surrounding archipelago. This bird is a member of a small but deeply interesting gallinaceous family known as the *Megapodinæ*, or great-footed birds, which have this peculiarity, that they never sit upon their eggs. They bury them in immense mounds that excite the astonishment of strangers, leaving them to be hatched by the heat of the sun or by fermentation. This family of birds is found in all the islands between Australia and the Philippines in one direction, and from Borneo to the Solomon Islands in the other.

A native went one day in search of the eggs of the *Megopadius tumulus*, as they are regarded as a delicacy. Whilst he was exploring the riches of a large mound, the upper part fell in and suffocated the poor fellow. So that it would be no exaggeration to say that this man was smothered in a bird's nest!

Beetles and butterflies are numerous and remarkably beautiful, as in the South Pacific.

CLIMATE.

Some of the islands—especially the elevated coral—are very healthy. The average reading of the thermometer over a large extent of Polynesia is about 80° Fahr. It seldom sinks lower than 60°. Owing to the smallness of most of the islands, and the prevalence of trade winds during the greater portion of the year, the heat rarely becomes intense. Still this constant heat and the moistness of the atmosphere are very debilitating to the European constitution. It is a remarkable fact that all the islands eastward of, and including, Fiji, are much more healthy than those to the west. Fever and ague are of rare occurrence in the eastern section, but of constant occurrence in the western. In New Guinea this fever becomes deadly. No wonder then that German New Guinea has been declared to be unfit for the residence of Europeans.

CYCLONES.

A large portion of the South Pacific is subject to destructive cyclones. The cyclone season is from December to the end of March. My own experience in the Eastern Pacific goes to show that a cyclone may be expected once in seven years. New Caledonia in the west, and the Society Islands in the east, are remarkably free from these visitations; but whenever they do come, they rage with appalling violence. The New Hebrides, &c., are visited by a more or less destructive cyclone nearly every year. Heavy seas invariably accompany them, exposing shipping to the gravest peril. Twice I have seen the storm-wave rising like a wall, 30 feet above the ordinary sea-level, and threatening to engulf the island. As it approached the shore, the awe-struck natives ran for their lives. To them it was the impersonation of an angry sea-god, Tane-ere-tue.

The terrible cyclone of March, 1889, at Apia Harbour (Samoa) will not readily be forgotten. Of seven war steamers lying at anchor, only one escaped. Upwards of 150 brave men then perished.

DISEASES.

Besides fever and ague (already referred to), the islanders are liable to dysentery, elephantiasis, hydrocele, lupus, and various skin diseases. Sometimes you see a middle-aged native spotted all over like a leopard, yet fairly healthy! Leprosy has been recently introduced, and is, I am sorry to say, spreading. The great curse of the islands undoubtedly is syphilis, introduced by Europeans. Measles and small-pox, unknown till a few years ago, have proved most destructive. In one island, within my own memory, the dead from small-pox, left unburied, were devoured by hogs! Wherever vaccination has been practised, the islanders have become the healthier for it.

RACES.

Two distinct races inhabit the South Pacific—the dark and the brown. The dark people inhabit the Western Pacific as far as, and including, Fiji. The brown people occupy the islands eastward of Fiji, as far as Easter Island, and southward as far as New Zealand. The brown race have founded a number of colonies among the dark people. In many instances these colonists, through intermarriage, have become almost as dark as the original inhabitants, still, however, preserving their own language and traditions. I have been greatly astonished on more than one occasion to find that I was able to speak freely in a Polynesian dialect to various colonists in the Western Pacific, who told me that their ancestors (two or three generations ago) had drifted from islands considerably more than a thousand miles to the eastward. The motive for sparing the lives of these strangers was the aid the males might render to the tribe that adopted them in the day of battle.

In New Guinea, from Redscar Bay eastward along the coast, as far, perhaps, as South Cape, there has been a considerable admixture of the brown (Polynesian) race with the original dark people. The inhabitants of Port Moresby and Hood's Point are much like Polynesians in colour (a little darker), manners, and even language. Let anyone conversant with Polynesian dialects carefully examine the dictionary of the Motu dialect, by the Rev. W. G. Lawes, and he will be convinced of the affinity that exists. It will be of great interest hereafter to learn exactly the relation these coast dialects bear to those of Polynesia.

My own impression is that the dark people north and south of Torres Straits were originally one; but that the vast difference of climate, food, &c., have made the present degraded aboriginals of Australia far inferior to their more favoured kinsmen of New Guinea. In Australia the coco-nut and sago palms were unkown until introduced by the white man.

THEIR ORIGIN.

In regard to the great Polynesian family, it is generally agreed among scientists that Baron W. von. Humboldt's theory is correct, viz., that they are of Malay origin. Hence they have been aptly called "Malayo-Polynesian." I believe that Samoa and Tonga were the groups first permanently occupied by the brown race. There is an air of refinement about those islanders, evident in their language as well as their manners, which we look for in vain in the eastern islanders. Besides, all the traditions of the eastern islands point to Samoa and Tonga as the original home of their ancestors and the starting-point of the great historical expeditions eastward in by-gone times. It is a curious circumstance that the name ("pororo") for "winter" in many of the eastern islands is confessedly derived from the Samoan name ("palolo") of an annelid* (prized as a delicacy) found only in Samoa and Tonga on the surface of the ocean, near the edge of the coral reef, in October and November of each year. So that whilst this annelid is not found eastward of Samoa, the time for its annual appearance is still indicated by the designation of the season of the year when it is due in the original home of the race. I may remark that the "l" in Samoan words is represented in all the islands eastward by the "r." My attention was first drawn to this by Taunga, the best living authority on the Rarotongan language, and who for thirty years was a much-respected pastor in the Samoan Group. In Samoa the season when it makes its appearance is known as "the time of palolo" ("vaipalolo").

* *Palolo viridis.*

The Samoan and the Tongans have a chief's language, also a high chief's language; so that virtually three dialects are simultaneously spoken by the same people. There is no trace of a chief's language in the Eastern Pacific, indicating that the Samoan and Tongan groups were the ancient seats of civilization. The antiquity of the civilization of the Samoans and Tongans, as compared with the Tahitians, Hervey Islanders, and New Zealanders, is attested by the fact that the latter have no word for "thanks," whilst the former have it ever on their lips. The Hervey Islander is silent on the reception of a gift; if he wishes to express gratitude, it must be by circumlocution.

The dark people of the Western Pacific and New Guinea are singularly deficient in historical traditions and poems which might assist us in forming a reasonable conjecture as to their origin. Of course, they possess shadowy traditions, but nothing that can be compared with the genealogies of the great ruling families of Polynesia. In view of this, I hesitate to venture a conjecture of mine own.

Certain it is that they occupy a much lower plane of civilization than that occupied by the brown race. In Fiji it is evident that the darker race has learnt much from the light-coloured, as it is well known that there has been a considerable admixture of the two races. It is, however, noteworthy that the dark people have from time immemorial excelled in the manufacture of coarse pottery, which the Polynesian race never attempted.

CLOTHING.

A narrow girdle is the only covering of the males of the dark race in the Western Pacific; but in many islands nothing whatever. In some islands this girdle is of plaited grass; in others of the inner bark of the paper-mulberry. In general, the women of the dark race wear a fringe around their loins. On Aneityum, Tanna, and Eramanga the females wore a petticoat, made by chewing the split aerial roots of the *Pandanus*. On Api the women used a tiny apron* of plaited grass, prettily stained, and secured by a string round the waist, the ornamental part hanging down. On Espiritu Santo the women, in 1863, wore mere tufts of green grass. To woman, in her lowest degradation, is given an instinctive modesty; but the men in heathenism are very different, "glorying in their shame."

The Polynesians were mostly a clothed race. The varieties of dress were numerous, each having a distinctive name. The paper-mulberry plant was extensively cultivated for that purpose. The inner bark of the bread-fruit tree was on some islands largely utilised for clothing. A wrapper or dress of this material is very pleasant and soft to wear, and of an agreeable light-brown colour. I have watched the preparation of a piece of a bread-fruit cloth, several hundreds of yards in length! Sometimes the bark of the banyan tree, of the *Hibiscus*, and even of that wonderful liana, the *Entada scandens*, furnished Polynesians (of the poorer sort) with useful clothing. On the atolls, where these fibre-producing trees and plants are unknown, the inhabitants have to be content with the split leaves of the *Pandanus* or the coco-nut, coarsely plaited. The women of the Line Islands, in 1863, wore an immense petticoat made of split pandanus leaves, reminding the visitor of the crinoline then in vogue amongst their fairer sisters in Europe and the States.

And now in regard to New Guinea. In 1872 I found the males of the dark Papuan race entirely nude; but the females wore a grass girdle extending from the waist to the knees. The males of the light-skinned tribes east of Redscar Bay wore an extremely narrow girdle (of paper-mulberry bark), or, as in the case of the Motu tribe, a string only; the women use grass girdles, ornamented by alternate red and yellow stripes of pandanus leaf. My first impression of the Redscar Bay women, in 1872, was that they wore some tasteful, close-fitting, lace-like garment; but it proved to be merely the exquisitely beautiful tattooing with which they were covered.

COMMERCE.

Prior to the introduction of Christianity, commerce did not exist. The commerce of the South Pacific and New Guinea may be now estimated at upwards of £3,000,000. So surely does civilization follow in the wake of Christianity. In those groups where Christianity has been fully established the value of the exports is about £5 per head. The principal exports are copra, pearl-shell, bêche-de-mer, cotton free from seeds, coffee, lime-juice, bananas, oranges, pine-apples, earth-nuts, arrowroot; and from New Guinea, red cedar, sago and spices.

MISSIONS.

Eighty years ago the whole of the Pacific was heathen. Now, upwards of 300 islands are Christianised. I first saw the Pacific in 1851. At that period the light was struggling with darkness. Visiting in 1862 most of the islands of the New Hebrides, there was scarcely one, save Aneityum, where the life of a stranger was worth five minutes purchase. To a large extent things are very different now; life and property are respected, the Sabbath is well observed, the Bible (or a portion of it) is read, and an industrious and peace-loving people are well clothed and hospitable to strangers. War, cannibalism, human sacrifices, systematic infanticide, &c., are things of the past, except in the Solomon Islands, &c., where little has been as yet done by missionaries. But even there the good work done by the Melanesian mission is not without its salutary influence over a considerable area.

Seven complete translations of the Scriptures have been made into dialects previously unwritten. Thirteen others are proceeding at the present moment. The Rev. W. G. Lawes has just carried through the press the entire New Testament in the Motu language spoken at Port Moresby, &c., in New Guinea. When, in 1872, the Rev. A. M. Murray and the writer first located native evangelists on the mainland of New Guinea, the existence of the Motu tribe was unknown to the civilized world; yet, to-day the Word of God is read and valued by many of those natives. That the message of Divine love should thus be conveyed in twenty barbarous dialects is itself a wonderful fact, whether regarded from a literary or a religious point of view.

A whole body of educational literature has sprung up in connection with mission work. The only attempt to make a collection of this sort of literature is that known in Auckland, New Zealand, as "The Sir George Grey Collection."

In 1797* the London Missionary Society commenced its work on the lovely island of Tahiti. The mission was subsequently extended over the Society and Austral Groups. The French occupation of those islands has very recently induced the London mission to transfer its work to the Paris Missionary Society with the utmost goodwill. The London mission still operates in the Hervey, Samoan, Tokelau, Ellice, and Loyalty Groups, and notably in British New Guinea.

King Pomare II. of Tahiti rendered invaluable assistance to the Rev. H. Nott in his admirable and thoroughly idiomatic translation of the Scriptures into the Tahitian language. The Tahitian version was the first of the many translations of the Bible into the languages spoken by the Pacific Islanders. The late Queen Pomare was the only daughter of this royal translator.

---

* The noble work done by my American brethren in the Sandwich Islands and other groups of the *North* Pacific scarcely falls within the scope of this paper, as I am writing only on the *South* Pacific and New Guinea.

In 1822 the Wesleyan Missionary Society began their work in the Tongan Group; in 1835 their work was extended to the Fiji Group; in 1877 they advanced to New Britain, New Ireland, &c.

The Presbyterians began work in the New Hebrides in 1848, amid a wild and treacherous population. On nearly all those once savage islands their missionaries are now labouring with marked success.

In that same year Bishop Selwyn first visited several of the islands in the Western Pacific. This led to the formation of the Melanesian (Episcopal) Mission. The tragic end of the lamented Bishop Patteson will be fresh in the minds of all readers.

A Roman Catholic (Marist) Mission was commenced in 1834 in the Gambier's Islands, and was afterwards extended to Tahiti, Marquesas, Samoa, Wallis' Island, Tonga and Fiji, New Caledonia and British New Guinea.

I once remonstrated with an incorrigible heathen thief on the peril to which he exposed himself by his tricks. He naïvely replied, " The day I was born my father dedicated me to Hiro, god of thieves. His servant I am. I know no other god. Why rebuke me for serving Hiro ? " This was in the Eastern Pacific.

In 1862 I first visited the Loyalty Islands (in the Western Pacific), and found a mission family with their converts in *nightly* expectation of a threatened attack from a host of cannibals. Years afterwards I again called, and found a well-clothed, industrious, law-abiding population, kind and courteous to strangers. A beautiful church (of large blocks of white coral) had been erected by these islanders for their own use. And, strangest of all, there was a band of twelve ex-cannibals, educated, and " mighty in the Scriptures," ready to go with the Rev. A. W. Murray and myself to instruct the heathen of New Guinea.

,

Notes oŋ the Ĥervey Islands, South Pacific.

(Annexed, at the request of the native chiefs, by Great Britain in 1888.)

BIRTH AND CHILDHOOD.

On the island of Mangaia, in the Hervey Group, as soon as a child is born, a leaf[*] of the *Alocasia Indica* (Seeman) was cut off, its sides carefully gathered up, and filled with pure water. Into this extempore baptismal font the child would be placed. First tying with a bit of "tapa" (native cloth made from the inner bark of the *Broussonetia papyrifera)* the part of the navel-string nearest the infant, the right hand of the operator *longitudinally* divided the cord with a bamboo-knife. The dark coagulated blood was then carefully washed out with water, and the name of the child's god declared, it having been previously settled by the parents whether their little one should belong to the mother's tribe or the father's. Usually the father had the preference; but *occasionally* when the father's tribe was devoted to furnish sacrifices, the mother would seek to save her child's life by getting it adopted into her own tribe, the name of her own tribal divinity being pronounced over the babe. As a rule, however, a father would stoically pronounce over his child the name of his own god—Utakea, Teipe, or Tangiia—which would almost certainly insure its destruction in after years. It was done as a point of honour ; besides, the child might *not* be required for sacrifice, although eligible. The bamboo-knife would be taken to the "marae" of the god specified, and thrown on the ground to rot. If a second god's name were pronounced over the child, the bamboo-knife would go to one "marae," and the name of the babe only be pronounced over the second "marae." The removal of the coagulated blood was believed to be highly conducive to health, all impurities being thus removed out of the system.

An analogy was believed to exist between the pith of a tree and the umbilical cord at birth. Hence the expressions "ara io" *i.e.,* "pathway of the pith," or simply "io"[†] *i.e.*, "pith," are still used for "God."

On the island of Rarotonga, when a boy was born, a collection of spears, clubs, and slinging stones was made. When the sun was setting, a leaf of that gigantic aroid, *Alocasia Indica,* filled with water, was held over these warlike weapons, and the umbilical cord treated as above described. The idea was that the child should grow up to be a famous warrior.

Infanticide was rarely practised in the Hervey Group, excepting at Rarotonga, where it was common.

In six out of seven islands of the Hervey Group cannibalism ceased only with the introduction of Christianity. It is worthy of note that on the remaining island—Mangaia—this revolting practice ceased *before* the introduction of Christianity, a circumstance unparalleled in Polynesia. It was in this wise: About a century before the Gospel was conveyed to those islands, the famous priest-chief, Mautara, had, by craft and force, crushed out all his foes, and seized the reins of government. There was not a person living on

---

[*] From 8 to 12 feet in circumference. The *Alocasia Indica* is a gigantic aroid, the native name of which is "kape."

[†] In Maori "iho" (=io) means the *funis umbilicus*. See "Myths and Songs" by the present writer page 37.

11

the island but was connected with him or his by worship, blood, or marriage. When this far-seeing man acquired absolute power, he wisely forbade cannibalism, through fear of perpetuating the anarchy which for generations had existed. Still the old habit showed itself again, even in Mautara; and solitary instances of cannibalism are known to have taken place in later times by stealth, not openly and constantly as in the early days of the celebrated priest-chief.

Old cannibal Hervey Islanders have assured me that human flesh is "far superior to pig." My worthy friend and helper, Maretu, of Rarotonga, was, in early manhood, a cannibal. This I learnt from his own lips. But the last generation that practised cannibalism has entirely disappeared. Their descendants, in many instances, through shame, deny the well-known facts of the past.

At Mangaia, and, I believe, the other islands of the Hervey Group. it was customary to prepare the body in this wise: The long spear, inserted at the fundament, ran through the body, appearing again with the neck. As on a spit, the body was slowly singed over a fire, in order that the entire cuticle and all the hair might be removed. The intestines were next taken out, washed in sea-water, wrapped up in singed banana leaves (a singed banana-leaf, like oil-silk, retains liquid), cooked and eaten, this being the invariable perquisite of those who prepared the feast. The body was cooked, as pigs now are, in an oven specially set apart, red-hot basaltic stones, wrapped in leaves, being placed inside to insure its being equally done. The best joint was the thigh. In native phraseology, "nothing would be left but the nails and the bones." It is worthy of notice that only warriors partook of these horrid feasts in the Hervey Group, very rarely, and by stealth, women and children (as in times of famine), or the remains of a broken clan hiding in the forest or in caves. Indeed, when a warrior wished his son to partake of human flesh for the first time, it was needful to deceive the lad by saying "it was only a bit of pork." Of course, when the truth oozed out, the son felt less scruple in following the evil ways of his father and uncles. Taoro, of Rarotonga, cooked his only child (a son) as a return feast for his cannibal friends. There can be no question that, at first, an inward voice protested against this unnatural practice. Yet, after a time, they learned to glory in their shame.

For many generations after the settlement of the islands cannibalism was rarely practised. Native traditions distinctly inform us when it was first sanctioned by the authority of leading men, and thus grew to be customary. Strange that on Mangaia it should again have ceased. In the opinion of many, in the deadlock which existed about the date of the introduction of Christianity, the natives of Mangaia would have relapsed into cannibalism. The deadlock was this:—Teaô would only consent to beat the drum of peace on condition that his two maternal uncles, the leading victorious warrior chiefs (Teaô being himself amongst the vanquished), were slain, and laid on the altar of Rongo as the price of peace! It was for this that Teaô lost his rank in after days.

Deformed children are very kindly treated indeed, although, perhaps, the deformity was occasioned by the cruel treatment of the parents in a burst of passion.

A single child is universally carried astride on the hip of the mother. "Thy daughters shall be nursed at thy side" (Isaiah, lx. 4). When there is a second child to be carried, it is placed on the shoulders of the mother, so that it rides triumphantly, holding on to the hair of the parent. This leaves one hip free to carry a basket of food and cooking leaves. It is rare for a father to carry his child.

I have known a lad, three years old, to be still suckled, but in general the period of suckling does not extend beyond two years. Too often infants are not suckled at all, on the plea that the "mother's milk is bad." Such children are "mama paru," *i.e.*, brought up by hand. Bits of "taro" (*Caladium petiolatum*), well chewed, are given to it from time to time. The kernel of an old coco-nut is finely scraped, the rich, oily juice is then expressed from it, and given in small quantities to the infant. The spoon anciently used for the purpose is the leaf of the *Gardenia*. I have often wondered how the stomach of the infants should be able to stand it ; but they do, and become fine men and women. Of late, however, the use of the coco-nut has gone out ot fashion, much to the detriment of the children. The soft, half-formed kernel itself is much used as the child becomes stronger.

Many natives feed their new-born children on "paka," *i.e.*, the baked leaves of the " taro,"; dipped in water. The mortality amongst infants thus reared is great, and should they attain to adult age they have a diminutive frame.

A chief's child would have three or four wet nurses, in order to produce the enormous frames for which they were famous.

It is customary for a native woman, when visiting her friend, to suckle her infant.

At Rarotonga, to regulate the shape of the child's head, it was a common practice to apply slabs of soft wood ("buka tea ") to the forehead and back of the head to produce the desired shape, *i.e.*, a high head. This practice did not obtain on Mangaia, nor, I think, on any other island of the Hervey Group.

It is still customary in the Hervey Group for mothers to press with the palm of the hand the noses of their infants, so that they may grow squat and round, "not (as I once overheard a woman say) like the *thin, starved* nose of the white race."

When children are small they are spoiled by their parents ; but when of a useful age all this disappears, and many of them have a very hard life. The curse of native family life is adoption ; this makes discipline almost impossible. A cross word will make the youngster run off to its adopted parents, who sympathise where they ought to scold. I have known parents take a present of food to the runaway, and humbly entreat his return ; but all in vain! These adopted parents, however, will resolutely set themselves to discharge the duties of real parents in teaching the youngster the arts needful in after life.

The betrothal of the female child often takes place in the families of chiefs, in order to secure a suitable match. In that case the girl is continually receiving presents from the family into which, at adult (say 13 or 14 summers) age, she is to marry. Should the contract not be fulfilled, full payment is exacted for all these gifts ; but, as a rule, the contracts are well kept, so many parties being interested in the affair.

MATURITY.

When circumcised, a lad considers himself to be a man. This rite was not unfrequently delayed, so that the lad might become a finer man. It was performed about the age of 17 or 18.

A Hervey Island girl may be considered mature at the age of 14. It must not be imagined that the ages of children were marked off by years, as with us.

For females, a slight tattooing, the patterns, being different from those on males, is usual.

She is expected to make her *début* by taking part in the next grand dance. The greatest requisites of a Polynesian beauty are to be fat and as fair as their dusky skins will permit. To insure this, favourite children in good families, whether boys or girls, were regularly fattened and imprisoned till nightfall, when a little gentle exercise was permitted. If refractory, the guardian would even whip the culprit for not eating more, calling out "Shall I not be put to shame to see you so slim in the dance?"

These dances invariably took place in the open air, by torchlight. About a year was required for getting up one such entertainment. This long interval was needed, first, for the composing of songs in honour of the fair ones, and the rehearsal of the performers; secondly, for the growth of "taro," &c., &c., to provide the grand feast necessary. The point of honour was to be the fairest and fattest of any young people present. I know of no more unpleasant sight than the cracking of the skin as the fattening process proceeds; yet this calls forth the admiration of the friends.

There is no analogy between the initiation of males into the tribe and the grades of freemasonry, it being done once for all. No new name is taken, no special colours used at the ceremony. The advantage that accrues is simply this—he ranks as a man, can marry, take part in tribal dances, songs, recitations, and the various duties of adult native life.

MARRIAGE.

Special messengers, of high social rank, are despatched to make the proposal and convey presents in ratification of the contract; but the betrothed child usually remains in the custody of its parents, now and then paying a visit to the other parties with much ceremony and under proper guardianship.

Marriage never occurs by force or capture. Sometimes a fallen tribe or family would endeavour to resuscitate its fortunes by giving in marriage the flower of the tribe to some disagreeable but powerful old chief.

The pet daughter of a chief often married into an inferior or fallen tribe, the parent intending thereby to swell the ranks of his own warriors by the welcome addition of this inferior or unlucky clan. In times of peace this servile son-in-law is expected to be at the beck and call of his father-in-law. There is, properly speaking, no such thing as sale or barter of wives in the Hervey Group.

Exogamy was the universal rule of the olden time. Should a tribe be split up in war, the defeated portion was treated as an alien tribe. I have known comparatively near relatives to marry with the approbation of the elders of the victorious portion of the tribe, expressly on the ground that the sanctity of the clan law had been wiped out in battle.

Distant cousins sometimes (though rarely) marry; but must be of the same generation, *i.e.*, be descended in the same degree (fourth or fifth, or even more remotely) from the common ancestor. That the male branch should thus invade the female is a far more pardonable offence than the converse, but even then, should misfortune or disease overtake these related couples, the elders of the tribe would declare it to be the anger of the clangod (kua kai te angai). It is the duty of parents to teach their growing children whom they may lawfully marry, the choice being extremely limited. The correct thing in the native mind undoubtedly is exogamy.

The nuptial ceremony consisted merely in a feast, when bride and bridegroom, seated together on a piece of the finest white native cloth,* ate together in the presence of their friends, and received gifts from them, the good things of the bridegroom's friends going to the bride, and *vice versa*.

---

* The inner bark of the *Broussonetia papyrifera* beaten out with mallets and pasted together.

A remarkable ceremony obtained on Mangaia in families of distinction on the marriage of the first-born. Gaily dressed, he walked from his own door-way to the house of the father-in-law over a continuous pathway of living human bodies, members of the wife's clan. On reaching the goal, three elderly females enveloped in the finest cloth, so prostrate themselves as to form a living seat for the bridegroom. A fish is now brought forward, and, with the aid of a bit of sharp bamboo, cut up into dice upon a human body. It is now presented to the bridegroom, who eats it raw. Piles of native cloth and food are then formally presented to the happy man. All parties partake of the feast, and afterwards the road of living bodies is again formed for the distinguished son-in-law to go back, as he came, to his home.

In due time (a few months later on) the husband's friends return the compliment to the bride, only it is understood that (unless of inferior social status) the second exhibition should surpass the first. The native name of this remarkable custom is " maninitori." It is a usage of great antiquity, but no account is given by tradition of its origin. (See my "Life in the Southern Isles," pp. 59, 60.)

Polygamy has been entirely done away with by Christianity. In the olden time it was very common, and was not restricted to chiefs. As women were rarely slain in war, superfluous females were divided out amongst the victorious warriors. The famous Arekâre, of Mangaia, had ten wives, Parima six, others two apiece. In general, if a man of position married the eldest girl of a slave-family, the younger sisters became his as a matter of course, being only too glad to have a protector. Even amongst those of equal rank, a man often had two or three sisters to wife at the same time. Even now, in Christian times, a woman feels herself to be deeply injured if her brother-in-law does not, on the death of his wife, ask her to become a mother to his children.

Children, unless distinctly adopted into another clan, always follow the father. The name of the god pronounced at the severance of the *funis umbilicus* really determines the clan of the infant, as before stated. In war they usually follow the father's kin ; but the duty of an adopted son would be to fight alongside of his adopted father. Sometimes serfs, forgetting the claims of blood, followed their lord to battle.

Land is the property of the tribe, and must on no account be alienated. The adopted son possesses land only so long as he goes with the clan, obeys the commands of the elders, and fights (if need be) against his nearest of kin for the tribe into which he has been adopted. A woman, in general, owns not an inch of soil, lest she carry away the right to it into another family. Usually she gives up one child at least to her own tribe, the rest going to the father's. When her husband dies, she lives on with the tribe as *slave* to her children. She weeds, plants, and eats because of them. If they die, she goes back to her tribe as she originally came—empty-handed.

When a chief has only a daughter, and that daughter is married (by the father's arrangement) to a man of inferior (*i.e.*, slave) rank. the husband lives with her on land given to her for their mutual support (or, as the phrase runs, "land given to her *to feed her husband*"). In all points *she* rules the household and lands ; but should war break out, *he* may elect to fight by the side of his father-in-law, and if victory incline to their side, he is no longer counted a slave. Should he go with his own clan to fight against his father-in-law's tribe, the wife may or may not go with him. Sometimes the wife, with her children, will stay on with her own clan ; so that, if victorious, the children will share the good things of the mother's tribe, whilst the unhappy father, if not slain in battle, becomes a homeless, hunted fugitive. In no case may a woman take into another clan any portion of the ancestral lands of her own tribe. The reason of this is obvious; these lands were originally won and subsequently kept by the bravery of the entire tribe. Rarely did women fight; their part was to stand a little behind the husband, to carry baskets of stones and weapons with which to supply the warriors. Heavy *tikoru* clothes were thrown by the wives over these spears to turn their points aside from the mark.

At Rarotonga, &c., the soil was the sole property of the high chiefs (ariki) and under-chiefs. These distributed the land in accordance with their own wishes.

I do not consider that orphans were in general ill-treated; the uncles, as a matter of course, looked after their welfare. In the native language there is but one word for "father" and "uncle." It was of the last importance to the tribe that their numbers should be kept up; hence the care taken of the children, and their careful education in mimic war.

There are no restrictions as to converse, but as to kissing ["rubbing of noses"] plenty. The rule is to "kiss" only *near* relatives on either side. The elders of the tribe settle these knotty points. Many a quarrel have I had to compose, the ground of the dispute being that the lady had no right to permit So-and-so to kiss her. The usual defence is, "it was done openly, and therefore could bear no ill significance." Half the troubles in native life arise from this source; the other half from land-grabbing, or, as the natives phrase it, "land-eating."

Woman is the slave of man in heathen society. She plants, carries home the food, collects the firewood and succulent oven-leaves, cooks her lord's meal, spreads out supper on hibiscus leaves (in lieu of plates, and of the same size), never omitting the sea-water, used as sauce and salt. Torch-fishing is woman's occupation only. Whenever she gets home, often in the small hours of the morning, a special oven for these dainties must be prepared by her for her husband and children. The wife is expected not only to feed but to clothe her husband. She strips off the bark of the paper-mulberry (*Broussonetia papyrifera*), steeps it in running water, beats it out with a square iron-wood mallet, pastes the strips together, stains the cloth, or, with the aid of leaves, makes designs on it, glazes the outer side, that her lord may strut about in his new clothes. *His* duty is to defend land and life, to plant and weed, and to fish with hook or net or spear. The wife, in her torchlight fishing, simply grabs sleepy fish, or puts her hand in holes which they haunt (often to her cost), but never uses either canoe, hook, or net.

But as their children (girls) grow up, all the duties of the mother are performed by the daughters. And the strange thing is, that they are perfectly content with their lot. To see a woman emerge from the mud of a taro-patch (up to her waist), in which she has been planting taro-tops (no man at Mangaia plants a taro-patch), and then go to the stream to wash herself, excites pity. But *she* does not think herself to need pity.

At Rarotonga, and some other islands, men plant and bring home the "taro," but the women weave mats and baskets.

After all, despite the horny hands of Mangaian women, their lives are pleasant, so long as Christianity secures immunity from the cruel bloodshed of heathen times. Even in the old time they enjoyed their dances and semi-dramatic performances. In general, it was the young women and girls who took part in these diversions, the middle-aged prompting or clapping hands or looking after the feast to follow.

The model Rarotongan warrior never (like other natives) allowed his wife · to *sleep on his arm*, lest his spirit should become enervated. After slaying a foe, he became "tapu," so that he might, for a certain period, only kiss his

16

wife and children. On no account might he cohabit with his wife until the "tapu" had been removed. During this period of "tapu," all the warriors of the same tribe lived together, receiving immense presents of food. When a sufficient interval had elapsed, in preparation for the removal of the "tapu," they would go unitedly to fish. If, while fishing, a warrior happened to be bitten by an "aa" (conger eel), or got his legs clasped by an octopus, he regarded this as a sure presage of a violent death. If he, that day, caught only a miserable fish, such as the poisonous "no'u," it plainly indicated that in his next battle he would only kill a wretched sort of person, not a chief or a warrior. On the other hand, if he caught a really fine fish, it was evident that he would hereafter conquer and kill some person of distinction, and thus enhance the fame of his tribe!

THE TRIBE.

Descent in the *male* line from a common ancestor (tama tane) constitutes the tribe. Descendants in the female line (tama vaine) *may* be adopted into the tribe, with the consent of the elders, after bathing in a sacred stream in order to wash off the taint of old slave or antagonistic associations. (See my "Historical Sketches of Savage Life," pp. 136-9). In general, slaves married into the victorious clans were content to follow its fortunes; but there were numerous exceptions to this rule. When dying, mothers of rank would commend their children to the chiefs of their own tribe, the slave-fathers having no voice whatever concerning their own offspring. The filial instinct, however, often led these children to endeavour to restore the fallen fortunes of the father's conquered clan. Usually, the question of tribe was decided by the divinity or divinities named at the severance of the *funis umbilicus*. But all the worshippers of Tanè, with its numerous modifications, were supposed to form but one tribe. In every case there must be oneness of origin (on the maternal if not on the paternal side), even in cases of adoption. When a great favour—life or land—was sought, it was wonderful how close the relationship was made to appear; but when a grudge had to be paid off, the sins (blood-shedding) of that branch of the clan were alone remembered.

Each tribe had its own god or gods,* its own "marae" or "maraes" (groves for worship), its own prayers and incantations, and its own songs. Even in the matter of clothing there were special differences. I have seen a man stripped naked for presuming to wear the garments of another tribe. The meek defence was that his grandmother was a member of the said tribe. Thus the will of the individual counted for nothing, or next to nothing, in heathen times.

There is one head chief, many subordinate ones. The office and power of chief is usually passed on to the brother, but when all the brothers were dead, would be transmitted to the eldest male branch of the eldest ruling family ("te kiko mua"). Whenever this individual was deficient in intellect or courage, the tribal oracle was sure to declare that the god had taken up his abode in another (generally speaking, the youngest male) member of ruling family. This divinely-favoured individual was then duly installed, and the entire tribe compelled to obey, as there could be no appeal from the word of the priest when inspired, for it was the fiat of the gods. On the island of Mangaia "Barima" was not the representative of the eldest branch of the tribe of Tanè, but he was undoubtedly the fittest man, specially selected, it was averred, out of his family by the god Tane-i-te-ata.

* The tribe of Ngariki worshipped Rongo, Ruler of Night, *i.e.*, the invisible world, and Motoro, one of the gods of "Day," or this upper and visible world.

Primogeniture was the rule, selection by the god the exception. The kingly office *might* descend in the *female* line; and this of necessity, as the males were so generally slain. But the male line would invariably be preferred.

The duties of a tribal chief were (1) to adjust disputes, (2) to confirm or lay aside wills (*viva voce* wills, of course), (3) to lead in battle, (4) to preside at all tribal work or feasting, (5) to provide at all points for the well-being of the clan, and (6) not the least important of a chief's duties was to consult or worship the gods, on his own behalf as chief and on behalf of the tribe. On Mangaia every high chief must worship Rongo, god of war and ruler of the invisible world. But there would be also his own private god, who must be duly honoured in the daily concerns of life. The worship of Rongo was reserved for great occasions, the making of war or peace, the selection of human sacrifices for the ratification of all degrees of chieftainship, &c. Summoned by the king, as high-priest of Rongo, all tribal chiefs were bound to attend, with a few followers, on behalf of their respective clans.

The State was conceived of as a long dwelling standing east and west; the chiefs of the southern (right) side of the island represented one side of it; the chiefs of the northern (left) side of the island represented the other side. The under-chiefs everywhere symbolised the lesser rafters; individuals, the separate leaves of thatch covering. Yet, by a subtle process of thought, the State itself—with its great and its lesser chiefs, and its numerous members—was but the visible expression of a spirit-dwelling in under-world, in which the major and minor divinities did not merely live, but actually constituted it; the major gods being the pillars and main rafters, the minor gods the lesser rafters, &c., &c. The safety of the State consisted in this— that in the spirit-temple in the nether-world there should be no schism or rent; for should there be one, divisions will immediately arise in the visible state, *i.e.*, in the councils of the great chiefs; the necessary consequences being war and bloodshed.

The order of descent in regal families was usually from father to son; but with great land or warrior chiefs it was different, the brothers of the deceased taking precedence of his sons, for the excellent reason that it was their strong arms that won or preserved the tribal lands. The kings were sacred men, priests of the great tutelar divinities; therefore, the representative of the senior branch in each generation was held in the greatest veneration, irrespective of age and sex, as being the visible mouth-piece and shrine of the invisible and immortal gods. But *no female* was competent to offer "prayers" (karakia), however well versed in them.

The elders and wise men of the tribe constituted the tribal council. The paramount chief or king must endorse their advice, else it was not law. It was the duty of the presiding chief to ask the opinion of the elders on any point.

Punishment for theft of food, was the destruction of everything edible on the land belonging to the family of the thief, or the taking of the culprit's life. In general, the former penalty was for members of the tribe; the latter for outsiders. In some islands all offences were punished with one— the death—penalty. No idea of proportion between an offence and its punishment existed in the native mind. As a rule, a chief might do any-thing he liked; not so the members of the tribe.

Polynesian chiefs were invariably fine men. Makea Daniëla, of Raro-tonga, would have been considered a very tall man, but for his extreme corpulence. He seemed to waddle, not to walk. In his infancy he had (as was usual with the children of high chiefs) three or four wet nurses at the same time. His eldest brother weighed 312 lb., their father nearly 5 cwt.

B

18

SOCIAL AND DOMESTIC.

In the Hervey Group the huts were in the form of a rectangle, and made of reeds. The thatch used by the common people was merely the plaited leaflets of the cocoanut palm—very pervious to rain. The idol temples and the great dwellings of the chiefs were covered with pandanus-leaf thatch—idol-temples first, dwellings of chiefs afterwards. The doors were always sliding. There was a sacred and a common entrance. Squares were prettily worked in black sennit on the front and back sides of the dwelling. The "tirango," or threshold, was made of a single block of timber, tastefully carved. *We* name our *dwellings* because they are enduring ; *they* name the *site*, their huts being so perishable.

Only the large open valleys of Mangaia and Atiu were cultivated in the olden time, but at Rarotonga a considerable portion of that narrow strip of rich soil, near the sea, was well planted.

The weeding spade of Mangaia was not unlike a club in shape, and was made of iron-wood (*Casuarina equisetifolia*). The length was 5 feet 9 inches. Indeed, it was a most formidable weapon at close quarters, as many an unfortunate has found to his cost.

The staff of life on Mangaia and Atiu is the "taro"* plant ; on Aitutaki, the sweet potato ; on Rarotonga, bread-fruit and plaintains ; on Mitiaro, &c., &c., coco-nut. In most of the islands a vast quantity of fish is eaten as soon as it is captured.

On Manihiki the natives subsist on coco-nut and fish : on the sister island of Rakaanga they have in addition a good supply of "puraka," *i.e.*, a coarse species of *Caladium*. On most of the atolls the inhabitants live contentedly on coco-nut and fish only.

Food is abundant throughout the Hervey Group except when a cyclone has wrought its desolation, or continuous rain has flooded the valleys where "taro" is cultivated.

About two days' work in a week will keep a plantation in good order. On atolls, like Manihiki, where only the coco-nut palm flourishes, no weeding or planting can be done, as the soil consists of sand and gravel thrown up by the ocean on the ever-growing coral. Hence it is that the natives of these atolls are such excellent fishermen, having little else to do.

The usual time for the one real meal of the day in the Hervey Group is at sunset. The richer natives have a warm meal about 10 a.m., but in general they cook enough at sunset to last for the morning's repast.

Throughout Polynesia the mode of cooking is similar. A circular hole, 2 feet or 3 feet in diameter, is dug in the ground, the centre being deeper than any other part. Firewood is split and piled up in the hole. Basaltic stones are now laid on the firewood just before it was lighted. When the fire had burnt out, and the red-hot stones fallen to the bottom amongst the glowing ashes, they are carefully arranged by means of a hooked green stick, of a sort that will not easily burn. A large bundle of succulent leaves are now thrown upon the hot stones, occasioning a dense cloud of steam to arise. On this the well-scraped "taro," split bread-fruits, sweet potatoes, or plantains are placed. Fish are invariably wrapped up in the leaves of the *Cordyline terminalis*, so that their juices may be retained. The oven is now covered in with a second bundle of fresh-plucked leaves. The dry leaves of yesterday are thrown on the top, and the whole pressed down by heavy stones kept for the purpose. In fine weather this steaming-oven was made in the open air, in rainy weather under shelter.

In heathen times it was customary at Mangaia and some other islands to slay all strangers. At Rarotonga, if a stranger landed in sight of one of

* *Caladium petiolatum.*

their kings his life was safe; but even then it was not quite wise to travel any distance in the bush without the chief. But in these days the stranger is fairly well treated, often far better than he deserves. He shares the good things going and remains as long as he likes. It is usual, on meeting another, to share whatever food may be in the hand or in the basket. The influx of visitors is rapidly producing a change in their customs; still, I think an unprejudiced observer must admit that the stranger is better cared for in Christian Polynesia than in Christian Britain. The generous man is the ideal good man yet.

Ear ornaments were universal. The shell of a species of coco-nut producing small, long nuts—their ends rubbed off on madrepore coral—were filled with fragrant flowers and leaves, and worn in the slit lobes of the ears of persons (males) of distinction. The lobes were marvellously distended by this practice.

The arms of warriors—between the elbow and the shoulder—were tattooed black only, so that, on dance nights, the beautiful white (*Ovula ovum*, Linn.) shell fastened across with sennit might be the more admired. Happy was the dancer who had a shell for *both* arms.

Just above the ankles finely-plaited hair was wound repeatedly, the amount indicating the rank and wealth of the wearer. So, too, with the wrists and neck. From the plaited hair on the neck of a chief was suspended a large pearl shell, or, in lieu of this coveted ornament, a piece of "miro" wood (*Thespesia populnea*), adzed into its shape. This plaited hair was called "manoa"; the breast ornament, "tia."

The ears of children were pierced with fish-bone, then enlarged with a twig of the gardenia, so as to admit a fresh-plucked flower (the scarlet *Hibiscus* or the *Gardenia*).

The women had to be content with necklaces and chaplets of flowers, but a favourite daughter might wear plaited hair round her neck. Of course, in each ear a flower was worn, and on her bosom a woman of rank might wear a "miro" ornament. Men emulated the other sex in regard to wreaths and necklaces, the latter often descending nearly to the knee. It is noteworthy that the septum of the nose was *never* pierced by the Hervey Islanders, as nasal ornaments were never in vogue in that part of the Pacific.

The Hervey Islanders were a clothed race. The inner bark of the paper-mulberry (*Broussonetia papyrifera*) yielded them the material for their "tikoru." Poorer natives were content to use the inner bark of the "aoa," or banyan tree. On Rarotonga, Aitutaki, and Mauke the inner bark of the bread-fruit tree yielded a light and beautiful garment. Even the *Entada scandens* was utilised by the poor for the manufacture of clothing.

The defect of native garments is their inability to keep out moisture. To remedy this, on Mangaia, the outside was sometimes anointed with scented coco-nut oil. The varieties of native dresses, with their distinctive names, were very numerous.

A native woman, in her own dwelling, wears a single garment—a petticoat. In the cold season she throws a "tiputa" over her shoulders. A man at work in the olden time, *i.e.*, when weeding, canoe-making, or fishing, wore only a girdle (māro). Travelling through the rain he was content with a girdle, but on arriving at his hut he would put on old warm clothing. A good covering of native cloth is (as I know from experience) as warm as a blanket.

An unmarried girl wore her petticoat nearly to the knee; when married, it was brought down just below the knee. In sitting, the Hervey Island females rested upon their heels, not, as in these days, tailor fashion. This latter indelicate custom was imported from Tahiti in recent times.

Speaking generally, it may be confidently stated that the natives are a well-nourished race. But in the old fighting days, when so small a portion of the soil was cultivated, it was hardly so. The chiefs and all the ruling race were indeed well nourished, but the "ao," or serfs, had sorry times of it. The frequent famines of those days were terrible. I have known natives who kept themselves alive on candle-nuts alone for months together; but they were wretched objects to look at. It is curious that a starved race becomes black almost, but if plenty returns, their natural, agreeable, coffee-colour is restored. In atolls, to the north-west of the Hervey Group and the Line Islands, the natives subsist chiefly on coco-nut, pandanus drupes, and fish. Should any accident (*e.g.*, if the leaflets are devoured by a plague of *Lopaphus coccophagus*, or a cyclone, or if the crowns are sprinkled by ocean spray) occur to the coco-nut palm, it is frightful to see the wasted forms of the islanders.

But even on the most fertile islands, after a cyclone, the sufferings of the natives are great. Happily, now, there are so many introduced plants, as well as imported food, that the natives do not perish of sheer starvation as in the days of heathenism. I have known entire families to subsist on the crown of a felled coco-nut, with what fish they could catch.

The salutation of the Hervey Islanders was the very reverse of our own. We bow to our friends; they toss the head upwards, at the same time elevating the eyebrows.

Their great national amusement was the dance. In this singular performance the joints seem to be loose. I do not believe it possible for any European to move the limbs as a Polynesian loves to do. At a very early age mothers carefully oil the hands, &c., and then knead the tiny limbs, stretching and "cracking" each joint. Respecting the *morality* of their dances, the less said the better; but the "upaupa" dance, introduced from Tahiti, is obscene indeed.

WIZARDS.

Priests *ex-officio* dealt with the gods and the invisible world. It was for them alone to approach the deities on behalf of the state, clan, or chiefs, *i.e.*, to chaunt *karakia* (prayers) at the "marae" * and present offerings. If Rongo were the divinity to be propitiated, a human sacrifice specially selected must be offered. To all other gods offerings of fish and "taro," &c., with the indispensable bowl of *piper methysticum*, were presented from time to time. No worshipper dared go empty-handed to his priest to inquire the will of the gods. The value of the gift must be proportioned to his rank and means. The load might be carried by male slaves to the outskirts of the "marae," but the offerer had a place allotted to him within the sacred precincts. The priest, or "god-box," clothed in white† *tikoru*, at a little distance, alone, in the most sacred place, went through the needful prayers.

In a case of sickness the deity would be asked about the fate of his devoted worshipper. At Mangaia the favourable response would be couched in these terms—"The spirit will go to the sun-rising" (ka acre ki te rā iti), *i.e.*, the sick will recover. For the spirit to descend with the sun-god Rā into the nether, or invisible, world is death. If the sufferer must die, a different metaphor was employed by the priest—"kua rau-ti para"—"The leaf of the *ti* tree (*Cordyline terminalis*) is sere," *i.e.*, will drop off and perish.

The office of priest was hereditary throughout the Hervey Group. When a new priest was installed, he first bathed in the sacred stream of his tribe,

* Idol grove.   † Off duty, the priest might wear a *yellow* "tiputa" over his shoulders.

put on the white *tikoru*, ate only certain kinds of food, and abstained from many things permitted to others. On the day of installation of the priest of Rongo the temporal chief accompanied him to the "marae"— not too closely following him. Offerings of food having been deposited at the usual spot, cooked "taro" and the invariable bowl of "kava" having been disposed of by the new priest-king, the temporal chief shouted "Ka uru Rongo"—" Let Rongo enter" (*i.e.*, inspire). The new high-priest, seated on a sacred stone,* then fell into convulsions, and spake in a most unearthly voice (? ventriloquism), the words so uttered being accepted as a divine oracle! Thus did the temporal sovereign install the new priest-king (*i.e.*, spiritual ruler). A grand feast would follow.

Less of ceremony was observed with priests of divinities of inferior rank, but substantially the same process was carried out. The technical phrase for this was "Va'i i te pia atua ou" = "open up the new god-box."

On the eve of an important battle "the omens were taken" (ka pa te vai) by the warrior chief himself. These omens consisted in the drowning of insects, &c., in water, or a fish hunt in the reef. (See my "Savage Life," page 104).

The native phrase, "Ka pa te vai," means literally, "enclose the water," because in taking the omens by the drowning of insects, &c., it was customary to arrange the cut stems of a banana in a square on the ground. A single leaf of the *Alocasia Indica* (Seeman), holding half a bucket of water, was deposited in the hollow, the water being kept from spilling by the cut banana stems. A number of centipedes, green lizards, and dragon-flies were now dashed into the water. The total of creatures drowned prefigured the number of warriors doomed to perish in to-morrow's battle. There was a special prayer (now lost) for this ceremony.

Sometimes two shells (*Turbo petholatus*), intended to represent the two hostile camps, were deposited by the warrior chief on his own "marae," with an appropriate prayer, in the dusk of evening. On returning at daylight, it is averred that Moke found the shell representing his foes turned upside down, a sure omen of their destruction, which accordingly took place.

On most of the eastern Pacific Islands were "wise women," who were consulted respecting the minor affairs of daily life. These women were supposed to be inspired by a female divinity. A small present must be made ere consulting the priestess. On Mangaia the goddess Ruatamaine was consulted to discover a thief, and to secure success in fishing. There were numberless Ruaatu, or fishermen gods (of stone) in all the islands, each demanding an offering of a newly-caught fish from its votaries, or, in default of that, a hollow pebble to be strung into a sort of necklace, or the midrib of a cocoanut leaf, and thrown into the darkness, with these words, "Here is thy share, O Ruaatu!"

The native name for sorcerer is "tangata purepure," *i.e.*, "a man who prays." A heathen only prays for the ill-luck or death of his foes. The prayers offered by the priests to the gods worshipped on the national or tribal "maraes" were termed "*karakia*"; those on minor occasions to the lesser gods were named "*pure*."† All these prayers were metrical,‡ and were handed down from generation to generation with the utmost care. There were "prayers" for every phase of savage life ; for success in battle ; for a change of wind (to overwhelm an adversary fishing solitarily in his canoe, or that an intended voyage of his own may be propitious) ; that coco-nuts, yams, &c., &c., may grow; that a thieving or murder expedition may be successful; that his hook or net may catch plenty of fish ; that his kite may

---

* Te koatu karakia=the stone for praying. † In New Zealand "*karakia*." ‡ Hence appropriately termed by us incantations.

fly higher than all others ; that his "teka" (reed) may outstrip the rest ; that
strong teeth may take the place of his child's first tooth when extracted. &c.,
&c. A great secret was the prayer at the excision of the *funis umbilicus*,
that the boy might be brave, or that the girl might in after-life be fruitful.
Few men of middle age were without a number of these prayers or charms.
They were usually uttered in too low a key to be heard by a stranger, lest
he, too, should thus be armed with a dangerous weapon of offence. If a
plantation were to be robbed, the appropriate prayer or charm must be
uttered near to it, so that it might have its full effect. If a man were to be
clubbed in his sleep, the prayer must not be used until the hut is in sight.
Important charms or "prayers" such as these were to grown-up sons part of the
equipment of life. In most cases, one or two would never be divulged until
there was a premonition of death in sickness or battle. A man felt that if
his last bit of "wisdom" were "reeled off" (to use a native parable), die he
must.

Payment to the sorcerer consisted in a couple of pieces of native cloth, or
fish and "taro," &c.

The succession was from father to son, or from uncle to nephew. So, too,
of sorceresses ; it would be from mother to daughter or from aunt to niece,
Sorcerers and sorceresses were often slain by the relatives of their supposed
victims.

A singular enchantment was employed to kill off the husband of a pretty
woman desired by someone else. The expanded flower of a *Gardenia* was
stuck upright—a very difficult performance—in a cup (*i.e.*, half a large
coco-nut shell) of water. A "prayer" was then offered for the husband's
speedy death, the sorcerer earnestly watching the flower. Should it fall, the
incantation was successful. But if the flower still remained upright, he will
live. The sorcerer would in that case try his skill another day, with perhaps
better success. Old natives assert that these enchantments, if persevered in,
never failed ; but that since the prevalence of Christianity they have all
become impotent. Indeed, the "prayers" themselves are happily lost.

In adzing a canoe, it was the duty of the chief taunga (artisan-priest) to
chant an extempore never-ending song, which the other workmen took up.
The song gave precision and unity to the stroke of their stone adzes, added
to their cheerfulness, and was believed to be supernaturally efficacious in
helping on the work to its completion. As the taunga would be sure to be
associated with the same set of helpers, the assistants knew pretty well what
was being chanted. This sort of thing was called a "pataratara"—"a
talking," of which I retain two written but untranslated specimens. Originally it was an address to the tree-spirit not to be angry at their adzing the
noble trunk, with an invocation to the axe fairy, Ruateātonga, to aid the
progress of the work.

Taraaere, the last priest of Tangaroa (who had often offered human sacrifices to the tutelar god of Rarotonga), when nearly ninety years of age, said
to me :—

"My father taught me how to retain wisdom (korero). He also told me
when to marry. He did not feed me with bananas, plantains, and fish, lest,
the food being light and slippery, wisdom should slip away from me. No !
he fed me with 'taro,' well beaten with a pestle, and mixed with cooked 'taro'-
leaves, the glutinous nature of the 'taro' being favourable to the retention of
wisdom."

This was uttered without a smile, in the full belief that this simple diet of
his youth and early manhood accounted for the marvellous memory which he
possessed to the very end of life. He assured me that it was thus the priests
of the olden days were brought up.

DEATH.

No one was believed to die a strictly natural death unless extreme old age was attained. Nineteen out of every twenty were regarded as victims of special divine anger or of the incantations of the "praying people" (Taugata purepure) *i.e.*, the sorcerers. Causes of death were:—

1. Infringement of *tapu* laws of all kinds.

2. An uttered resolve broken ; *e.g.*, preparation for battle upon the receipt of false intelligence. The trick may be seen through after a time, still the fight must at all risks come off, if once the war-girdle has been put on. Not only would shame attend the withdrawing warriors, but the special wrath of the war-god would rest upon them. So that there is nothing for it but fight at all risks. A journey prepared for, but not carried out. Many years ago it was 'intended that the writer should remove to Rarotonga to take charge of the mission there. Everything was ready, when a brother from England arrived for that station. It so happened that just afterwards I lost two sons in one week of diphtheria. I was astounded to find that the natives of Mangaia, while sympathising with my loss, attributed the sad blow to my failure to carry out my original purpose.

3. A grave dug for a corpse, but not occupied. At the last moment perhaps the owner of the soil objects to the burial, so the corpse is disposed of elsewhere. In that case, the natives firmly believe that someone else must die in order to occupy the empty grave.

4. Unusual luxuriance of growth of plantations of food. The saying is, " E mou Avaiki tena," *i.e.*, " it is also a crop for spirit-land " (portends a crop for the reaper Death, as *we* perhaps would phrase it.)

The bodies of deceased friends were anointed with scented oil, carefully wrapped up in a number of pieces of cloth, and the same day committed to their last resting-place. A few were buried in the earth within the sacred precincts of the appropriate "marae;" but by far the greater number were hidden in caves regarded as the special property of certain families.

If a body were buried in the earth, the face was invariably laid downwards, chin and knees meeting, and the limbs well secured with strongest sinnet cord. A thin covering of earth was laid over the corpse, and large heavy stones piled over the grave. The intention was to render it impossible for the dead to rise up and injure the living! The head of the buried corpse was always turned to the rising sun, in accordance with their ancient solar worship.

It was customary to bury with the dead some article of value—a female would have a cloth-mallet laid by her side ; whilst her husband would enjoin his friends to bury with him a favourite stone adze, or a beautiful white shell (*Ovula ovum*, Linn.) worn by him in the dance. Such articles were never touched afterwards by the living.

Numbers were buried in caves easily accessible, to enable the relatives to visit the remains of the dearly-loved lost ones from time to time. The corpse was occasionally exposed to the sun, re-anointed with oil, and then wrapped in fresh *tikoru* (white native cloth).

The dead were never disembowelled for the purpose of embalming. The corpse was simply desiccated, and daily anointed with coco-nut oil. A month would suffice for this.

Warriors were in general hid by their surviving friends, through fear of their being disinterred and burnt in revenge.

The people of the entire district where the deceased lived take up " taro " and prepare a feast in honour of the dead. A grand interchange of presents is usual on these occasions ; but, excepting the near relatives of the deceased, no one is really the worse for it, as it is etiquette to see that distant relatives get back similar articles to what they brought.

Whatever is laid upon the corpse is buried with it, and no further notice taken of it ; but whatever is placed by the side, without touching it, is repaid.

The moment the sick died, the bodies of near relatives were cut with sharks' teeth, so that the blood might stream down the bodies ; their faces were blackened, and the hair cut off. At Rarotonga it was usual to knock out some of the front teeth in token of sorrow. Everywhere the moment of death was the signal for the death-wail to commence. The most affecting things are said on such occasions, but always in a set form, commencing thus :— "Aue tou e! Aue! Aue!"—Alas for us! Alas! Alas! &c. The wailers usually lose their voices for several days, and their eyes are frightfully swollen with crying.

As soon as the corpse was committed to its last resting-place, the mourners selected five old coco-nuts, which were successively opened, and the water poured out upon the ground. These nuts were then wrapped up in leaves and native cloth, and thrown towards the grave ; or, if the corpse were let down with cords into the deep chasm of " Auraka," the nuts and other food would be successively thrown down upon it. Calling loudly each time the name of the departed, they said, " Here is thy food ; eat it." When the fifth nut and the accompanying "raroi," or pudding, were thrown down, the mourners said, " Farewell! we come back no more to thee."

A death in the family is the signal for a change of names amongst the near relatives of the deceased.

Chiefs and priests occasionally receive the honour of a " spirit-burial," the corpse being borne to the most renowned "marae" of his tribe on the island, and allowed to remain within the sacred enclosure for some hours, but the same day hidden away in the tribal cave. In such cases the depositing of the body in the "marae" was " the burial," or the committal of the spirit to the care of the god worshipped in life, whilst the letting down of the corpse into the deep chasm was designated " the throwing away of the bones " (tiringa ivi), the well-wrapped-up body being regarded as a mere bundle of bones after the exit of the spirit.

In the olden times, relatives of the deceased wore only "pakoko," or native cloth, dyed red in the sap of the candle-nut tree, and then dipped in the black mud of a taro-patch. The very offensive smell of this mourning garment was symbolical of the putrescent state of the dead. Their heads were encircled with chaplets of mountain fern, singed with fire to give it a red appearance.

The era, or dirge, and the mourning dance succeeded. Of this dirge, four varieties are known. They invariably took place by day, occupying from ten to fifteen days, according to the rank of the deceased. Sometimes a " death-talk " was preferred, consisting of sixty songs in honour of the dead, mournfully chanted at night in a large house built for the purpose, and well lighted with torches. Each adult male relative recited a song. A feast was the inevitable finale.

Each island of the Hervey Group had some variety of custom in relation to the dead. Perhaps the chiefs of Atiu were the most outrageous in mourning. I knew one to mourn for seven years for an only child (a woman), living all that time in a hut in the vicinity of the grave, and allowing his hair and nails to grow, and his body to remain unwashed. This was the wonder of all the islanders. In general, all mourning ceremonies were over in a year.

SPIRIT WORLD.

Spirit-land proper is underneath, where the sun god Rā reposes when his daily task is done. It is variously termed Po (Night), Avaiki, Hawai'i, Hawaiki, or home of the ancestors. Still, all warrior spirits, *i.e.*, those who have died a violent death, are said to *ascend* to their happy homes in the ten heavens above. *Popularly*, death in any form is referred to as "going into night," in contrast with day (ao), *i.e.*, life. Above and beneath are numerous countries and a variety of inhabitants—invisible to mortal eye; but these are but a *fac-simile* of what we see around us now.

The Samoan heaven was designated Pulotu or Purotu, and was supposed to be under the sea. The Mangaian warrior hoped to "leap into the expanse," "to dance the warrior's dance in Tairi" (above), "to inhabit Speck-land (Poêpoê)" in perfect happiness. The Rarotongan warrior looked forward to a place in the house of Tiki, in which are assembled the brave of past ages, who spend their time in eating, drinking, dancing, or sleeping. The Aitutakian brave went to a good land (Iva) under the guardianship of the benevolent Tukaitaua, to chew sugar-cane for ever with uncloyed appetite. Tahitians had an elysium named "Miru." Society Islanders looked forward to "Rohutu noanoa," *i.e.*, "sweet-scented Rohutu," full of fruit and flowers.

At Mangaia the spirits of those who ignobly "died on a pillow"* wandered about disconsolately over the rocks near the margin of the ocean, until the day appointed by their leader comes (once a year), when they follow the sun-god Rā over the ocean, and descend in his train to under-world. As a rule, these ghosts were well disposed to their own living relatives; but often became vindictive if a pet child was ill-treated by a step-mother or other relatives, &c. But the esoteric teaching of the priests ran thus:—Unhappy† ghosts travel over the pointed rocks round the island until they reach the extreme edge of the cliff facing the setting sun, when a large wave approaches to the base, and at the same moment a gigantic "bua" tree (*Fagræa Berteriana*), covered with fragrant blossoms, springs up from Avaiki to receive these disconsolate human spirits. Even at this last moment, with feet almost touching the fatal tree, a friendly voice may send the spirit-traveller back to life and health. Otherwise, he is mysteriously impelled to climb the particular branch reserved for his own tribe, and conveniently brought nearest to him. Immediately the human soul is safely lodged upon this gigantic "bua," the deceitful tree goes down with its living burden to nether world. Akaanga and his assistants catch the luckless ghost in a net, half drown it in a lake of fresh water, and then usher it into the presence of dread Miru, mistress of the nether world, where it is made to drink of her intoxicating bowl. The drunken ghost is borne off to the ever-burning oven, cooked, and devoured by Miru, her son, and four peerless daughters. The refuse is thrown to her servants, Akaanga and others. So that, at Mangaia, the end of the coward was annihilation.

At Rarotonga the luckless spirit traveller who had no present for Tiki was compelled to stay outside the house where the brave of past ages are assembled, in rain and darkness for ever, shivering with cold and hunger. Another view is, that the grand rendezvous of ghosts was on a ridge of rocks facing the setting sun. One tribe skirted the sea margin until it reached the fatal spot. Another (the tribe of Tangiia, on the eastern part of Rarotonga), traversed the mountain range forming the backbone of the island until the same point of departure was attained. Members of the former tribe clambered on an ancient "bua" tree (still standing). Should the branch chance to break, the ghost is immediately caught in the net of "Muru." But it sometimes happens that a lively ghost tears the meshes and escapes for a while, passing on by a resistless inward impulse towards the outer edge of the reef, in the hope of traversing the ocean. But in a straight line from the shore is a round hollow, where Akaanga's net is concealed. In this the very few who escape out of the hands of Muru are caught without fail. The delighted demons (taae) take the captive ghost out of the net, dash his brains out on the sharp coral, and carry him off in triumph to the shades to eat.

For the tribe of Tangiia an iron-wood tree was reserved. The ghosts that trod on the green branches of this tree came back to life, whilst those who had the misfortune to crawl on the dead branches were at once caught in the net of Muru or Akaanga, brained, cooked and devoured!

Ghosts of cowards, and those who were impious at Aitutaki, were doomed likewise to furnish a feast to the inexpressibly ugly Miru* and her followers.

Evidently the ancient faith of the Hervey Islanders was substantially the same. Nor did it materially differ from that of the Tahitian and Society Islanders, the variations being such as we might expect when portions of the same great family had been separated from each other for ages.

There is no trace in the Eastern Pacific of the doctrine of transmigration of human souls, although the spirits of the dead are fabled to have assumed, temporarily, and for a specific purpose, the form of an insect, bird, fish, or cloud. But gods, specially the spirits of deified men, were believed permanently to reside in, or to be incarnate in, sharks, sword-fish, &c., eels, the octopus, the yellow and black-spotted lizards, several kinds of birds and insects. The *Ignis fatuus*, opportune mists concealing a victim, imagined balls of fire guiding the fleeing or killing party, were all the working of their gods for the destruction, safety, or guidance of mortals.

In sleep, the spirit was supposed to leave the body and travel over the island, to hold converse with the dead, and even to visit spirit-world. Hence, the dreams of mortals. Some of the most important events in their national history were determined by dreams.

The place in which the placenta (enua) of an infant is buried is called the "ipukarea," or natal soil; and it was believed that, after death, spirits of adults, as well as children, hover about the neighbourhood.

MYTHOLOGY.

Strictly speaking, the Hervey Islanders had no conception of a creator, as the islands were believed to be dragged up out of the depths of Avaiki, or Nether-World, otherwise called Po, or Night. These islands are merely the gross outward form, or body; whilst their still remains behind in the obscurity of Nether-World the ethereal essence or spirit.

The primary conception of the Hervey Islanders as to existence is a *point*; then something *pulsating*; next, something greater—*everlasting*.

The universe is to be conceived of as the hollow of a vast coco-nut shell, the interior of which is named Avaiki. At the very bottom of this supposed coco-nut shell is a thick stem, gradually tapering to a point, which represents the very beginning of all things. This point is a spirit named *The-root-of-all-existence*. Above this extreme point is another demon, named *Breathing, or Life*, stouter and stronger than the former one. The thickest part of the stem is *The-long-lived*. These three stationary, sentient spirits constitute the foundation, and insure the permanence and well-being of all the rest of the universe.

---

* The goddess *Miru* of Mangaia and Aitutaki is the *Muru* of Rarotonga.

In the interior of the supposed coco-nut shell, in the lowest depths of Avaiki, lives a woman, or demon, of flesh and blood, named Vari-ma-te-takere (shortened into Vari)—*The-very-beginning*. At various times Vari plucked off three bits from each side, and moulded them into human shape. These six are the primary gods of the universe. Yet no "marae" or image was ever sacred to them, nor was any offering ever made to them.

The first of the six primary gods is Avatea or Vātea (Noon), half man and half fish, whose eyes are the sun and moon.* Evidently we have in Avatea, or Vātea, the god of light. The second primary god is Tinirau (Innumerable), the lord of all fish. The third is Tango (Support). The fourth is Echo (Tumuteanaoa), regarded as a female dwelling in hollow rocks. The fifth, Raka, or Trouble, presides over winds. At the edge of the horizon are a number of wind-holes. To each child is allotted one of these apertures, through which he blows at pleasure. The sixth and last of the primary gods is a female, Tu-metua, or Tu-papa, who dwells with the Great Mother. "Vari." at the very bottom of Avaiki, in the *Silent-land*, the only language of which is that of signs and smiles, to comfort her. Tu† (short for Tu-metua or Tu-papa) was the tutelar goddess of the island of Moorea. To her the fourteenth night in every moon was sacred.

In his dreams, Vātea, the eldest of the primary gods, saw a woman, Papa (Foundation), whom he afterwards succeeded in making his wife. Now Papa was the daughter of Timātekore (Nothing-more). Tangaroa and Rongo‡ were the twin children of Vātea and Papa. They were the first beings of perfect human form in the universe, and possessed no second shape. Three other sons (Tonga-iti, Tangiia, and Tane-papa-kai) were born to Vātea and Papa. These are the principal deities of the Hervey Islanders and (and with numerous variations and additions) of Eastern Polynesia. To the children of Vātea and Papa belong the maraes and idols; they received the offerings and listened to the prayers of mankind.

The tutelar god of Mangaia is Rongo, whose wife Tākū bore him a daughter named Tavake. The boast of the three original tribes on Mangaia is that they are the descendants of Tavake by her own father Rongo, *i.e.*, that they are of divine origin,

Now, Rongo was likewise the dread deity of Tahiti and the Leeward Islands, under the slightly modified designation of "Orō." The original marae of "Orō" in Eastern Polynesia was Opoa, on the island of Raiatea, whence the worship spread to all the neighbouring islands.

At the shrine of this deity, on the island of Tahiti alone, fifty reeking heads were offered in a single generation. To Rongo, Orō, Rono, or Orono (as he is variously named), no offering was acceptable but a bleeding human sacrifice, specially selected. males being always preferred to females. At Tahiti females were ineligible, being regarded as "noa" (common); whereas males where "tapu" (sacred), and therefore suitable for sacrifice.

Tangaroa was specially honoured at Rarotonga, Aitutaki, Samoa., and the Society Islands. In the Tahitian and Society Groups, Ta'aroa was regarded as the originator of the world, and the parent of gods and men. At Samoa, Tangaloa was regarded as the great creator.

The gods were divided into two orders, "dwellers in day," and "dwellers in the shades, or night." The former busied themselves with the affairs of

---

* The moon is the fish-eye, on account of its paleness.

† When Captain Cook, for the second time, visited Tahiti, he found the king to be "Otoo," ancestor of the present Pomare. "Otoo" should be written Tu, the O being a mere prefix to all proper names. This mythological name was adopted in order to secure for its owner the reverence due to the gods, who are invisible to mortal eye.

‡ In the Society Islands "Orō" (Ro[ng]o) was the son of Ta'aroa (Tangaroa) not his twin brother.

mortals, moving, though unseen, in their midst; and yet often descending to Nether-World, the true home of the major-gods. The latter frequently ascend to-day to take part in the affairs of mankind, but prefer to dwell in spirit-land (night). A few were supposed to remain permanently in the obscurity of Avaiki.

Many of the deities worshipped in the Hervey Group and other islands of the Eastern Pacific were canonised priests, kings, and warriors, whose spirits were supposed to enter into various birds, fish, reptiles, insects, &c., &c. Strangely enough, they were regarded as being in no respect inferior to the original divinities.

The gods first spake to man through the small land birds; but their utterances proved to be too indistinct to guide the actions of mankind. The gods were thus led to communicate with mankind through the medium of a human priesthood. Whenever the priest was consulted, a present of the best food, accompanied by a bowl of intoxicating "piper methysticum," was indispensable. The offerer, in a stentorian voice, said, "Ka uru Motoro"—Enter (i.e., inspire), Motoro!* At these words the priest would fall into convulsions, the god Motoro having inspired (literally, "entered") him, and the oracle would be delivered. From the oracle thus delivered no appeal whatever lay. The best kinds of food were sacred to the priests and chiefs.

Although unsuited for the delivery of oracles, birds were ever the special messengers of the gods to warn individuals of impending danger, each tribe having its own feathered guardians.

The great Polynesian word (Atua) for "God" means strictly *the pith core, or life of man.* This is evident from its constant equivalent, "ara io," shortened sometimes into "io," which literally signifies "pathway of the pith," or "pith." What the pith is to the tree, the god is to the man, i.e., *its life.*

The greater gods alone had carved images for the convenience of worshippers; the lesser were countless, each individual possessing several.

PHILOLOGY.

A list of numerals and pronouns in the language, with suggestions as to their etymology :—

NUMERALS.

1	...	...	Okotai, tai
2	...	...	Rua.
3	...	...	Toru
4	...	...	A.
5	...	...	Rima.
6	...	...	Ono.
7	...	...	Itu.
8	...	...	Varu.
9	...	...	Iva.
10	...	...	Ngauru.
11	...	...	Ngauru ma tai (10+1).
12	...	...	Ngauru ma rua (10+2), &c.
20	...	...	Rua ngauru (2+10).
21	...	...	Rua ngauru ma tai (2+10+1).
22	...	...	Rua ngauru ma rua (2+10+2), &c.,
100	...	...	Anere (i.e., from the English "hundred") &c.

* Or whatever may be the name of the worshipper's deity.

In the Hervey Group we have two distinct bases of numeration—four and ten. The former base is used in counting coco-nuts, which were from time immemorial tied up in four (kaviri).

5 Bunches (kaviri) of coco-nuts make one Takau, *i.e.,*			20
10 Takau	„	„ Rau	200
10 Rau	„	„ Mano	2,000
10 Mano	„	„ Kiu	20,000
10 Kiu	„	„ Tini	200,000

All beyond this is uncertain.

PRONOUNS.

1.—*Personal.*

First person	Au ...	... Mana ...	Matou
First person, including the second	...	... Taua ...	Tatou
Second person	Koe ...	... Korua ...	Kotou
Third person	Aia, ia ...	... Raua ...	Ratou

Of the dual and plural pronouns of the first person, "taua" and "tatou" include the person or persons spoken to, while "maua" and "matou" exclude them.

2.—*Relative.*

Tei and nona, nana.

"Tei" is used only in the past tense, and becomes "te" in the future, and is generally accompanied with "ka."

3.—*Adjective.*

First person singular	Toku, taku
Third person singular	Tona, tana
First person plural	To matou, ta matou, &c.

4.—*Interrogative.*

Koai	Who
Teica	Where
Eaa	What
Teea	Which

Koai and teica are declinable.

5.—*Demonstrative.*

Singular
- Teia ... ... This
- Teianei ... ... This here
- Tena ... ... That (near the person spoken to)
- Tera ... ... That (at a distance)

Plural
- Eia ... ... These
- Eianei ... ... These here
- Ena ... ... Those (near the person spoken to)
- Era ... ... That (at a distance)

6.—*Indefinite.*

Etai, tokotai ... ... Some, few

Paradigm of the conjugation and declension of the verb "to go" and of the verb "to kill," with a pronominal object :—

Aere ... Go

Indicative Mood.

Singular.	Dual.	Plural.
Pres.—Te aere nei au ...	Te aere nei maua ...	Te aere nei matou, &c., &c.
Past—I aere ana au ...	I aere ana maua ...	I aere ana matou, &c., &c.
Fut.—Ka aere au	Ka aere maua	Ka aere matou, &c., &c.

Imperative.
Ka aere koe, &c.

Subjunctive or Conditional Mood.
Present—Me aere au, &c.
Past—Naringa au i aere.
Future—Kia aere au.

Infinitive.
E aere.

Participle.
Aere anga.

Ta ... ... Strike, kill*

Indicative Mood.

Singular.	Dual.	Plural.
Pres.—Te ta nei au, &c....	Te ta nei taua, &c. ...	Te ta nei tatou, &c.
Past—I ta ana au, &c. ...	I ta ana taua, &c. ...	I ta ana tatou, &c.
Fut.—Ka ta au, &c. ...	Ka ta taua, &c.	Ka ta tatou, &c.

Imperative.
Ka ta koe.

Subjunctive or Conditional Mood.
Present—Me ta au, &c.
Past—Naringa au i ta, &c.
Future—Kia ta au, &c.

Infinitive.
E ta.

Participle.
Ta anga.

Indicative Mood (Passive Voice).

Singular.	Dual.	Plural.
Pres.—Te taia nei au, &c....	Te taia nei taua, &c.	Te taia nei tatou, &c.
Past—I taia na au, &c. ...	I taia na taua, &c....	I taia na tatou, &c.
Fut.—Ka taia au, &c.	...Ka taia taua, &c. ...	Ka taia tatou, &c.

Imperative Mood.
Ka taia koe, &c.

Subjunctive or Conditional Mood.
Present—Me taia au, &c.
Past—Naringa au i taia, &c.
Future—Kia taia au, &c.

* When a native wishes to say " kill," he uses this phrase, " Ta kia mate "—" Strike, so that (he) may die ;" or "Ta ua." Still, " ta " may by abbreviation mean:' kill."

A few simple sentences to show the grammatical structure of the language:—

Eaa tena?	What is that?
E noo ki raro	Sit down
E tu ki runga	Get up
Aea koe aere ei?	When will you go?
Apopo	To-morrow
Kapikiia	Call (him)
Teia, te aere mai nei	Here he comes
Koai toou ingoa?	What is your name?
E vaine taau?	Are you married?
E tamariki taau?	Have you any children?
Tokoia?	How many?
Kua maki koe?	Are you ill?
Ka mate paa koe	You will perhaps die
Kare rava ia	Not a bit of it
Man	Tangata
Woman	Vaine
Head	Upoko, mimiti (of animals)
Hair of head	Rauru
Eye	Mata
Nose	Putaiu, putangiu
Tongue	Arero
Ear	Taringa
Hand	Rima
Thumb { Mangaia	Nui, (i.e., big)
{ Rarotonga	Maikao maata (big finger)
Foot	Vaevae
Bone	Ivi
Blood	Toto
Fire	A'i
Water	Vai
Sun	Ra
Moon	Marama
Father	Metua tane
Mother	Metua vaine
Son	Tamaroa
Daughter	Tamaine
Brother (of a woman)	Tungane
Sister (of a man)	Tuaine
Cousin	Taeake
Uncle	Metua tane
Aunt	Metua vaine
Give	Omai; orouga mai
Take	Rave atu
Make	Anga
Bear	Apai, maranga
Burn	Ka
See	Akara
Hear	Akarongo

As an illustration of their genius and mode of thought, I subjoin a song composed before the introduction of Christianity; also five ancient myths—one from Tahiti, two from Aitutaki, two from Mangaia, and one from Rakaanga.

A SONG FROM THE ISLAND OF MANGAIA.

In the early part of the year 1815, Enuataurere, the eldest daughter of the warrior chief Rakoia, was accidentally drowned at Tamarua, on the southern part of the island of Mangaia, in the Hervey Group. A few months afterwards my worthy old friend—according to the custom of the ruling families—solaced himself by chanting her praises in a song composed by himself at a grand *fete* in honour of the deceased. Enuataurere was at the time of her death about fifteen years of age.

Long years afterwards Rakoia named my only daughter Enuataurere, after his own lost child. On this occasion the venerable chief chanted this song in the presence of the elders of the clan, as a formal adoption of the child. At various times Rakoia crossed the island, spear in hand (not for battle, but as a support to his failing limbs), to bring presents of food to his adopted daughter, invariably chanting this song in praise of Enuataurere.

Rakoia, at the period of his death in 1865, was about eighty years of age. He had, ere Christianity had been introduced, fought in four pitched battles, besides several minor engagements. He was accounted the best poet of his day. The following is the song, written down from his lips :—

THE PRAISES OF ENUATAURERE.
BY RAKOIA; CIRCA A.D. 1815.

Taū tama nei ! Eaa rai ē !
Uri mai koe i te inangaro kimikimi,
Kia akataataa, e taū ariki.
E au maiku tcia ē !

My First-born ; Where art thou?
Oh, that my wild grief for thee,
Pet daughter, could be assuaged !
Snatched away in time of peace.

Ua kau koe ia maveiiti
I te tapu o te ariki.
O piri tau o ange karetu o te vao :
E tiere rau kokovi ē !

Thy delight was to swim,
Thy head encircled with flowers,
Interwoven with fragrant laurel
And the spotted-leaved jessamine.

Tei ia oki tooku inangaro,
Tei pau atu na iaau.
E korero tuku na te metua ;
Akairi ake i reira ē !

Whither is my pet gone—
She who absorbed all my love—
She whom I had hoped
To fill with ancestral wisdom ?

Na ara puātou, na ara kakea ;
E motu ai to aerenga 'tu i te avatea.
E uu maire, eaa mai o te rā ē !

Red and yellow pandanus drupes
Were sought out in thy morning rambles,
Nor was the sweet-scented myrtle forgotten.

E apinga ua i pukea mai,
Ka apai na te ao roi toka piri.
Ua puipui te puka 'i—
Ei iaaku koe, naaku rava,
I tu ake taū inangaro ē !

Sometimes thou didst seek out
Fugitives perishing in rocks and caves.
Perchance one said to thee,
" Be mine, be mine for ever ;
For my love to thee is great."

Manea metua i te tupa-anga i te tama ē !
O Ennataurere ! O Enuataurere !

Happy the parent of such a child !
Alas for Enuataurere ! Alas for Enuataurere !

E kaura nga Tapairu :
Ei matareka no Enuataurere ē !

Thou wert lovely as a fairy?
A husband for Enuataurere !

Ua mataano to tangata e,
Ei iaku koe ē !

Each envious youth exclaims,
" Would that she were mine !"

O Enuataurere i te tai kura i te moana.
Te nunga koe i te uru o te kare i tai ē !

Enuataurere now trips o'er the ruddy ocean.
Thy path is the foaming crest of the billow.

Aue ē ! Enuataurere ē !
Enuataurere ē !

Weep for Enuataurere—
For Enuataurere.

The most interesting stanza is the last but one—

Enuataurere now trips o'er the ruddy ocean.
Thy path is the foaming crest of the billow.

The spirit of the girl is believed to follow the sun, tripping lightly over the crest of the billows, and sinking with the sun into the underworld (Avaiki), the home of disembodied spirits.

THE COCO-NUT TREE.—A TAHITIAN MYTH.

AT Tahiti lived a king named Tai (Sea), who wedded the lovely queen Uta (Shore). She had lived with her husband for some time, when a great longing came over her to visit the relatives she had left behind in the home of her youth. But the king did not like her to go without a fitting present. He therefore inquired of the oracle what would be most suitable. The god directed him to send his wife to a certain stream, and tell her to watch for the coming of an eel; that she should catch the first that presented itself, cut off its head, and deposit it in a calabash and carefully plug up the aperture. The body of the eel was then to be thrown back into the stream, and the calabash carried to the husband.

Upon Uta's return from the stream, the king inquired whether she had carried out the instructions of the oracle. The wife joyfully said yes, and laid the well-plugged calabash at his feet. Tai now directed her to start on her intended journey, and present the precious calabash to her parents and brothers, "for there is wondrous virtue in it." He told her that it would grow into a coco-nut tree, and would bear a delicious fruit never before seen. He enjoined her on no account to turn aside from the path, nor to bathe in any tempting fountain, nor to sit down, nor to sleep on the road, and above all not to put down the calabash.

Uta gladly started on her journey. For a while all went well, but, at length, the sun being high in the heavens, she became very hot and weary. Perceiving a crystal stream, she forgot her promise to her husband, put down the calabash, and leapt into the inviting waters. After disporting herself for some time in the cool stream, she cast a glance at the calabash, but, lo! it had sprouted—the eel's head had become a young tree with strange leaves! Grieved at her own folly, she ran to the bank and strove with all her might to pull it up, but could not, for its roots had struck deep.

Uta wept long and bitterly. Perplexed now what to do, with joy she perceived a little messenger-bird from her husband directing her to return. She went back to the king with shame and fear, and related to him all that had befallen her. Tai sadly said to her, "Go to the stream into which you cast the body of the eel, whose head was placed in the calabash; find the wriggling tail, and destroy it by beating it with a stick, then come back and tell me."

Uta did as she was desired; but as soon as she entered their dwelling her husband expired in expiation of her sin.

RATA'S CANOE.—A LEGEND FROM AITUTAKI.

IN the fairy land of Kupolu* lived the renowned chief Rata, who resolved to build a great double canoe, with a view of exploring other lands. Shouldering his axe, he started off to a distant valley where the finest timber grew. Close to the mountain stream stood a fragrant pandanus tree, where a deadly combat was going on between a beautiful white heron and a spotted sea-serpent. The origin of the quarrel was as follows:—

The heron was accustomed, when wearied with its search after fish, to rest itself on a stone rising just above the waters of the coral reef, and chanced to defile the eyes of a monstrous sea-serpent whose hole was just beneath. The serpent, greatly enraged at this insult, resolved to be revenged. Raising its head as far as possible out of the water, it carefully observed the flight of the white heron and followed in pursuit. Leaving the salt water of the

* This is the "Upolu" of the Samoan Group.

C

reef, it entered the mountain torrent, and eventually reached the foot of the fragrant pandanus, on a branch of which the unconscious victim was sleeping. The sea-serpent easily climbed the pandanus by means of one of its extraordinary ærial supports or roots; and now, holding on firmly with its twisted tail, began the attack by biting the lovely bird. .

They fought hard all through that night. At dawn, the white heron seeing Rata passing that way plaintively called out, "O Rata, put an end to this fight." But the serpent said deceitfully, "Nay, Rata, leave us alone; it is but a trial of strength between a heron and a serpent; let us fight it out." Again the white heron begged Rata to interfere; and again the crafty sea-serpent bade Rata to go on his way—which he did, being in a great hurry to fell timber for his canoe. But as he walked heedlessly along, he heard the bird say reproachfully, "Ah! your canoe will not be finished without my aid." Still Rata heeded not the white heron's cry for help, but entered the recesses of the forest. Selecting the finest timber he could find, he cut down enough for his purpose, and at sunset returned home.

Early on the following morning the chief returned to the valley, intending to hollow out the trees he had felled on the previous day. Strangely enough, the logs were missing; not a lopped branch, or even a chip or a leaf could be seen! No stump could be discovered, so that it was evident that the felled trees had, in the course of the night, been mysteriously restored to their former state. But Rata was not to be deterred from his purpose, so having again fixed upon suitable trees, a second time he levelled them to the ground.

On the third morning, as he went back through the forest to his work, he noticed that the heron and the serpent were still fighting. They had been thus engaged for two days and nights without intermission. Rata pursued his way, intending to hollow out his canoe, when, to his astonishment, as on the previous day, the fallen trees had resumed their original places, and were in every respect as perfect as before the axe had touched them. Rata guessed, by their position and size, which were the trees that had twice served him this trick. He now for the first time understood the meaning of what the suffering white heron had said to him on the first day, "Your canoe will not be finished without my aid."

Rata now left the forest and went to see whether the white heron was still alive. The beautiful bird was indeed living, but very much exhausted. Its unrelenting foe, sure of victory, was preparing for a final attack, when Rata chopped it in pieces with his axe, and thus saved the life of the white heron. He then went back to his work, and for the third time felled the timber for his canoe. As it was by this time growing dark, he returned home to rest.

From the branch of a distant tree the somewhat revived white heron watched the labours of Rata through the livelong day. As soon as the chief had disappeared in the evening, the grateful bird started off to collect all the birds of Kupolu to hollow out Rata's canoe. They gladly obeyed the summons of their sovereign, and pecked away with their beaks until the huge logs were speedily hollowed out. Next came the more difficult task of joining together the separate pieces. The holes were bored with the long bills of the sea birds, and the sinnet was well secured with the claws of the stronger land birds. It was almost dawn ere the work was completed. Finally, they resolved to convey the canoe to the beach, close to Rata's dwelling. To accomplish this, each bird—the small as well as the large—took its place on either side of the canoe, completely surrounding it. At a given signal, they all extended their wings, one to bear up the canoe, the other for flight. As they bore the canoe through the air they sang, each with a different note, as follows:—

E ara rakau ē! Eara rakau ē!	A pathway for the canoe! A pathway for the canoe!
E ara inano ē!	A path of sweet-scented flowers!
E kopukopu te tini o Kupolu._	The entire family of birds of Kupolu
E matakitaki, ka re koe! Ōō!	Honour thee (Rata) above all mortals! Ōō!

On reaching the sandy beach in front of Rata's dwelling, the canoe was carefully deposited by the birds, who now quickly disappeared in the depths of the forest.

Awakened by this unwonted song of the birds, Rata hastily collected his tools, intending to return to his arduous employment in the valley. At this moment he caught sight of the famous canoe, beautifully finished off, lying close to his door. He at once guessed this to be the gratitude of the king of birds, and named the canoe "Tarai-po," *i.e., Built in a night, or Built in the invisible world.*

ECHO; OR THE CAVE FAIRY.—A LEGEND FROM MANGAIA.

THE first king of Mangaia was named Rangi, who had previously dragged up the island from the depths of the unseen world. Rangi resolved to explore every nook and corner of his new realm, to ascertain whether there were any other inhabitants in his territory.

After travelling some distance along the northern division of his domains without discovering the slightest trace of any living creature, he approached a romantic pile of rocks overhanging a tremendous gorge, by which the waters of the neighbouring valleys discharge themselves into the ocean. A number of caves converge at this point, the pathway to which is obstructed by vast boulders.

Here Rangi shouted, as was his wont, "Ōō" ("Hallo, there!"). To his surprise a voice from the rocks distinctly replied, "Ōō." Rangi asked, "What is your name?" Instead of a satisfactory reply came the defiant query, "What is *your* name?" Rangi, bursting with indignation, now demanded of this unseen fellow-resident, "Whence do you come?" Still the invisible speaker declined to reveal herself, and the ears of Rangi were assailed with the irritating words, "Whence do *you* come?" Unable to endure this any longer, he cursed the hidden inhabitant of the cave, nicknaming her "Aitu-mamaoa," *i.e., the ever-distant,* or *the-hide-and-seek spirit;* but forthwith heard himself cursed in exactly the same tone and words. Evidently this satirical, unseen being was no respecter of persons. Rangi fell immeasurably in his own estimation.

Rangi now resolved, at any cost, to get a sight of the insolent creature pertinaciously hiding in the rocks. Cautiously leaping from boulder to boulder, he entered the gorge, inquiring as he proceeded for the hitherto invisible inhabitant, but receiving for his pains only sarcastic replies. The chasm grew darker and narrower, but Rangi kept bravely on his way. Upon suddenly looking up, to his astonishment, he found that the arched roof was everywhere covered with transparent glittering pendants (stalactites), white, like a row of formidable teeth, almost touching his person, drops of cold water meanwhile falling like rain upon a stone flooring. Underneath was a row of stumps (stalagmites), rising up from the basement of the cave. Awe-stricken at the sight of these vast open jaws, apparently about to swallow him up, he instinctively retreated a few steps, and, looking up once more, for the first time caught a glimpse of the face of a female fairy, heartily laughing at his terror.

As soon as Rangi recovered his equanimity, he inquired the proper name of this formidable apparition. Her reply was, "I am Tumuteanaoa, or Echo" (literally, "the cave-speaking sprite"). "I am the being that everywhere inhabited the rocks of Mangaia ere you set feet on the soil."

The cave where Rangi first made the acquaintance of Echo, was thenceforth named Aitu-mamaoa, or the home of the ever-distant, or hide-and-seek spirit.

In the course of his subsequent exploration Rangi often met with this notable nymph Echo, who seemed to be ubiquitous. No difficulty ever arose from the presence of Echo in his dominions, as she was a nymph of a gentle and harmless disposition, her only fault being that she was a little satirical when addressed by strangers.

MAUI THE GREAT.—An Aitutakian Myth.

THE great Māui, who had eight heads, formerly lived in utter darkness in Avaiki, or nether-world. On one occasion, as he was wandering about in his gloomy abode, he saw a faint streak of light issuing from a small aperture in the roof. Māui at once conjectured that there must be somewhere beyond a world of light, and resolved at any cost to leave the dark prison-world which he had always inhabited. He tried hard to reach the hole, and succeeded in doing so ; but, upon endeavouring to squeeze himself through, found it impossible, on account of the number of his heads. Without hesitation Māui plucked off one of his heads, and vainly tried again. A second head was plucked off ; but, though he possessed now only six, he could not get through. True to his resolve to explore the realms of day, Māui deprived himself of the sixth, fifth, fourth, and third heads. "Now," thought this god of the shades, "having but two heads left, I shall be sure to get through." He tried, and once more failed. Off went one of the remaining heads, and the hero entered the narrow hole ; and, to his great delight, speedily emerged into a flood of light in this world of ours. Nor did he ever regret the sacrifice he had made to attain so rich a reward ; for he made this world his permanent home. Hence it is that now all mankind, his descendants, have but one head apiece !

DELUGE—MYTHS.—From Mangaia.

ORIGINALLY the surface of Mangaia was everywhere a gentle slope from the centre to the sea, without a single depression or valley ; and the following is the account given of the process by which the island was changed to its present condition :—

Aokeu,* a son of Echo, disputed warmly with Ake who should perform the most wonderful thing. Ake's home is the ocean, and his constant employment to tread down its flooring ; thus ever deepening its vast basin, and enabling it to contain more of his favourite element. Ake was confident that he could easily beat Aokeu, who was ignobly born of the continual drippings of purest water from the stalactite roof of a narrow cavern.

To insure success, Ake summoned to his assistance Raka, fifth child of the great mother, Vari—originator-of-all-things. Raka, as god of winds, complacently drove a fearful cyclone over sea and land, as though about to bury the island for ever. Tikokura and Tane-ere-tue, twin children of the god of winds, also lent their willing aid ; the former being impersonated in

---

* Aokeu = "Red-circle," alluding to discolouration of the ocean after heavy rains.

the huge curling line of breakers which in bad weather threatens to shiver the solid coral reef to atoms; the latter in the rarely-seen storm-wave, which never fails to strike terror in the heart of the spectator.

On rushed these mighty monsters, sure of victory. They actually succeeded in covering the highest rocks near the shore, about 100 feet above the level of the sea. As a lasting memorial of this achievement, numberless clam and other shells, as well as *ungakoa*, or "coral-borers," are to this day firmly embedded in the solid rock,* which is burrowed and worn—even at its highest points—into a thousand fantastic shapes by the action of the sea.

Meantime, Aokeu had not been idle. He caused the rain—his favourite element—to fall, without the slightest intermission, five days and nights in dreadful torrents. The red clay and small stones of the interior were washed into the ocean, discolouring its waters to a considerable distance. Still the rain poured down with unabated violence. On every side the channels deepened, until the narrow valleys of the interior were formed; and as the storm went on, the larger valleys near the sea, walled in on the seaward side by perpendicular rocks, and now the principal taro-planting districts, gradually assumed their present dimensions. The flat summit of the central hill, Rangimotia, "the crown of Mangaia," was alone uncovered with water, to indicate what the original height of the interior had been.

At the outset, Rangi, the first sovereign of Mangaia, had been warned of the desperate strife of elements about to take place ; and, with his few people, awaited at Rangimotia the issue of the contest. It was with great concern that he saw, on the one hand, the wild ocean covering the belt of rocks which surrounds the island, and, on the other hand, a vast lake of fresh water rising rapidly, and tumultuously rushing to meet the advancing ocean. Everywhere an immense expanse of water met the eye of Rangi, save only the long and narrow strip of level soil upon which he and his people tremblingly stood. Already the water had reached their feet. What if it should rise a little higher ? Rangi resolved to appeal to Great Rongo to save him and his beloved "Auau" (Mangaia) from destruction. To reach his marae, then facing the rising sun, it was needful for the brave Rangi to make his way through the waters, which reached his chin, along a ridge of hills to a point named Teunu, lying due east. Just here is a spot still called "the standing-place of Rongo," because that divinity at once accepted the petition of his grandson ; and, looking at the fierce conflict going on—the floods of the interior meeting, and raging against the waters of the ocean— he shouted, "A tira !" (it is enough) : a phrase then for the first time used, but in after times scarcely ever off the lips of mortals.

The eye of Vātea (*i.e.*, the sun) too, opening at that moment above the scene of conflict, saw and pitied mankind. The ocean sullenly returned to its former level, and the rain ceased ; after a while the waters of the interior were drained off, and the present agreeable diversity of hill and vale was eventually presented. Hence the proud name of the supreme god of Mangaia, *Rongo arai kea*, *i.e.*, "Rongo, the warder-off of mad billows."

Mankind were saved ; and the land became better adapted than ever for their residence. Aokeu, lord of rain, was acknowledged victor ; for after the wild rage of ocean had expended itself upon the rocky heights near the sea, the appearance of the cliffs remained essentially the same ; and the fierce sons of the god of winds had, after all, failed to reach the interior of the island. But the turbid floods rushing down from the central hill extended far away into the ocean, everywhere marking their triumphant progress with the red clay of the mountains of Mangaia.

---

* Hardened coral, upheaved by volcanic agency in some remote period of the earth's history.

D

To this famous contest Koroa refers in his fête-song in memory of Tekaire, *circa* A.D. 1818.

Akaotu te ngaru,
E tei te moana ae ē!

Chorus.
The demon of the billows
Is disporting himself in mid-ocean.

Te riri o Vātea.

Solo.
Such is the might of Vatea.

Vaere atu i te poue
I te paepae o Rongo ē!
O Rongo arai mai i te kea ē!

Chorus.
Clear away the wild vines
Invading the precints of Rongo's grove.
'Tis Rongo who wards off the mad billows.

And again, in the same song:

Nga taae a kutu mai a kutu ē!

Chorus.
These surf-gods are for ever thundering

Ae ē!

Solo.
Aye!

Te kutu nei nga maoata,
Kua reru aere i te ngangie
I te mato i te raei ē!
O Rongo arai mai i te kea ē!

Chorus.
These angry sea-gods are ever at work,
Breaking down and crashing the trees;
E'en climbing the rocks and high cliffs.
'Tis Rongo who wards off the mad billows.

It was so real a contest in the estimation of men of former days, tha opinions were divided as to the route actually taken by Rangi in making fo the marae of Rongo (formerly in the east, but afterwards removed to the west). Some asserted that it was by the direct path terminating at Vivitaunoa others thought that, to avoid the dip beyond Vivitaunoa, Rangi traversed th south-eastern ridge terminating at Paeru.

This myth stands alone, no other achievement being attributed to Aokeu which is a proof of its antiquity.

FROM RAKAANGA.*

A KING named Taoiau† was on one occasion greatly incensed against hi people for not bringing him the sacred turtle. The irate chief "awakened all the mighty sea-gods upon whose goodwill the existence of the islands-Rakaanga and Manihiki—depends, particularly a great divinity who sleeps a the bottom of mid-ocean, and who, at the prayers of Taoiau, rose up in ange like a vast upright stone. A dreadful cyclone began, and the ocean ro and swept over the entire island of Rakaanga. The few inhabitants of tho days escaped destruction by taking refuge on a mound which was pointed on to me. This memorable event is known as "the overwhelming of Taoiau."

In Indian story, Menu, or Mānu, is the Noah whose boat floated in safe over the waters which drowned the world. "Mānu" is the great Polynesia word for floating on the surface, as of a thing submerged. "Mānu" is t universal word for bird, *i.e.*, as floating or gliding through the air. Is t similarity merely accidental?

---

* A low coral island lying between the Samoan and Hervey Groups.
† Taoiau = peace-bearer.

Sydney : Charles Potter, Government Printer.—1892.